# THE COST
*of*
# LIVING

Text copyright © Margaret Cundiff 2000

The author asserts the moral right
to be identified as the author of this work

Published by
**The Bible Reading Fellowship**
Peter's Way, Sandy Lane West
Oxford OX4 5HG
ISBN 1 84101 137 1

First published 2000
10  9  8  7  6  5  4  3  2  1  0

**Acknowledgments**
Unless otherwise stated, scripture quotations are taken from
the Good News Bible published by The Bible Societies/
HarperCollins Publishers Ltd, UK © American Bible Society
1966, 1971, 1976, 1992, used with permission.

Extracts from the Authorized Version of the Bible (The King
James Bible), the rights in which are vested in the Crown, are
reproduced by permission of the Crown's Patentee, Cambridge
University Press.

Extracts from The Book of Common Prayer of 1662, the rights
of which are vested in the Crown in perpetuity within the
United Kingdom, are reproduced by permission of Cambridge
University Press, Her Majesty's Printers.

Extract from *The Alternative Service Book 1980* is copyright ©
The Archbishops' Council, and is reproduced by permission.

Extract from CPAS *Family Service* leaflet is copyright © CPAS
1968, 1976, and is reproduced by permission.

A catalogue record for this book is available
from the British Library

Printed and bound in Great Britain by
Caledonian Book Manufacturing International, Glasgow

# THE COST
*of*
# LIVING

*A personal journey in*
*John's Gospel Chapters 11–21*

# *Margaret*
# CUNDIFF

*For Peter,*
*with love and thanks*
*as we celebrate*
*our forty years of marriage*

# Contents

# By way of explanation

Why did I choose to write about these chapters from John's Gospel—chapters 11 to 21, the second half of the Gospel?

They portray so vividly the cost of living the Jesus way of life. Jesus raises his friend to life and starts on the road to Calvary, which for him is death, then life. The road he takes is the road we must take, towards our own death; and if we will accept this gift, it is the road to life.

These chapters are, for me, exciting, compelling, demanding. But there are two difficulties. Unlike the Gospel of Mark, which is very plain, direct reading that almost anyone can understand (and that is why it is so often chosen to give to new Christians), John's Gospel has within it great theological argument, which is all of a piece with the narrative. So those with little background of Christian teaching may read about the events but miss out on the deep truths which are so vital for them. On the other hand, for Christians who know their Bibles, the words are so familiar that they too are in danger of missing their inner meaning.

I am trying to meet both groups. I want those who know these chapters so well to look at them in the light of the world we live in, the harsh realities of the beginning of the twenty-first century. I want those who are almost totally caught up with today's world and its problems to turn and look at Jesus, and walk the road with him to death and to life. I want us all to meet the characters, hear the debates, witness the natural and supernatural events, and not to be afraid of those who say, 'Oh yes, but there's more to it than *that*!'

I like to think I am travelling the road with both groups, adding my comments, sharing how I feel and how certain situations remind me of my own experience; and being forced to forget my preconceived ideas and be open to what Jesus has to say to me on the road.

So who is the book for? Anyone who is willing to walk with me! I hope that what I write will be from the heart as well as from the head, and will remind me that I have to make up my own mind about the issues of life and death. I have to be willing to see things in a new light, and I may have to alter my views on some things. I find it exciting—I hope others will, too.

As you are reading this book, you will find it helpful to read also the relevant passages from John's Gospel—preferably in the Good News Bible translation, but if you do not have this, any version will do. I have given the appropriate reference at the head of each of my chapters.

*Margaret Cundiff*

# CHAPTER I

# Point of no return

## JOHN 11:1–16

There are events in our lives which, when we look back at them, we can see were both ends and beginnings. Each was a moment of decision, which affected every other moment from then on—a small step, as it seemed at the time, which left behind all that had gone before and put the seal on all that was to come. It may have been the way we answered a question or responded to someone's need. It could have been an action taken on the spur of the moment, or after agonizing thought and discussion—an emotional response or, in the cold light of day, the result of calculating the pros and cons of a certain course of action.

When did Jesus take the step that made the cross inevitable? At what stage in his life did he 'burn his boats'?

You could say that in one way there was never a choice at all; but to say that is to deny the reality of free will, the gift of the Father to his Son as much as to us. Without free will we would be robots, mere puppets on strings, responding only to the tugs and whims of the Heavenly Controller, dancing to his tune, incapable of personal response. God the Father gave to Jesus his Son, his heir of earth and heaven, freedom of the universe. He came to this earth as a baby, yet with the status of Lord. He 'came of age' when he came to earth. He was free to decide, to act and to reap the result.

There are many ways to choose from, many paths to follow, yet in the final analysis only two. The way of life or the way of death... but life or death for whom?

Jesus was always in danger, a fugitive. From his birth he was on the run. As a babe in arms his parents had to carry him away to Egypt for safety. Herod, in anger and fear, had his squad of butchers murder all the baby boys of two years and under in the Bethlehem area because the infant Jesus was a threat to his plans; and Jesus continued to be a threat to those who would use power and prestige for their own ends. Time after time Jesus escaped by the skin of his teeth—or by the grace of God—from the hands of violent men. He was always a threat as long as he was alive; the only way he could be contained was by destroying him, removing him from the scene.

Yet there were times of peace and security for Jesus. Times when, away from those who aimed to destroy him, he was sought out by those who looked for the secret of life, of health, of peace. These were ordinary people for the most part, called 'common' people—because there were so many of them! They were those who had open minds and open hearts.

So we see Jesus, having escaped from the dangers of Jerusalem across the River Jordan, enjoying a period of successful ministry, preaching, teaching and healing. People were responding to him. Many of them had been prepared by John the Baptist and were ready in heart and mind for Jesus, in whom they recognized the one whom John had promised. Some may have witnessed the baptism of Jesus by John. They accepted Jesus with love.

Success at last! A growing support, a safe haven—things were on the up and up!

Then a message arrived for Jesus. It was a very simple message, sent from some friends of his, two sisters who loved him and who looked to him in their need now. Their brother Lazarus was desperately ill. No one could help him—no one except, as the sisters Mary and Martha knew, their family friend Jesus. Yet he was much more than a family friend. He was the Lord and Master; for the message was 'Lord, your dearest friend is ill.' Just that. No demands, no suggestion as to what Jesus should do, how he should respond; just the facts of the situation. Maybe they did not ask him to come because they knew that it would put him in danger. It could have been that they did not ask him to come because they knew that distance made no difference to his love and power. They just put the facts before him.

What options had Jesus got? To rush immediately to Bethany, responding as fast as possible. To ask his Father to heal Lazarus—after all, he did not have to be physically present at the bedside of Lazarus to heal him. He had no need to put himself in danger by going to see Lazarus. He could have sent a messenger with words of sympathy for the sisters. Or he could have decided that his place was to be with the people who were responding to his message where he already was. After all, what was one person's need compared with the crowds?

He did... nothing. He talked about the result of the illness not being final—meaning death. He spoke of what had happened bringing glory to God, and also of its being the means of his glory; but he did nothing. For two days he did nothing. No message, no action—nothing.

Have you ever waited for two days for something to happen? For a letter, a phone call, a visit? Have you ever sat by the bedside of someone very ill for two days, when nothing seemed to happen one way or the other? Have you ever suffered pain, loneliness, depression, anxiety, fear, or anything else for two days? Two days can seem like a lifetime. Two days when nothing happens are an eternity, when heaven and earth stand still, when we are suspended out of time, out of life.

What was Jesus thinking about for two days? What were his friends thinking about—those who had heard the message? And what about the messenger?

Then Jesus announced his decision—'Let us go back to Judea.' He would go to his friend Lazarus. He would go, as he said, 'to wake him up'. He was going in his own time, the right time.

In the Old Testament, the book of Ecclesiastes (which means 'The Preacher') describes in very poetic language that everything has its right time.

*Everything that happens in this world*
*happens at the time God chooses.*
*He sets the time for birth and the time for death,*
*the time for planting and the time for pulling up,*
*the time for killing and the time for healing,*
*the time for tearing down and the time for building.*
*He sets the time for sorrow and the time for joy,*
*the time for mourning and the time for dancing,*
*the time for making love and the time for not making love,*
*the time for kissing and the time for not kissing.*
*He sets the time for finding and the time for losing,*
*the time for saving and the time for throwing away,*
*the time for tearing and the time for mending,*

*the time for silence and the time for talk.*
*He sets the time for love and the time for hate,*
*the time for war and the time for peace.*

**Ecclesiastes 3:1–8**

Yes, there is 'the right time' for everything. This was plain in the ministry of Jesus. He sought his Father's time, the perfect time.

We want things in our time, and that time is usually 'now'—for we live in a world which knows only 'now'. Ours is a society of instant coffee, and the instant answer; a microwave society, which has satisfaction on demand, done just right: almost as the thought enters the head it is expected in the hand. So when, instead of an immediate answer to our prayers, we hear only the sound of our own voice, we either panic, shout and scream, jump up and down like demented figures on space invader games, or we arrogantly pronounce judgment: 'There is no God, there is no answer; we have proved it so.'

Our lives are governed by time, our time—the days, the hours, the minutes, the seconds. We surround ourselves with reminders of time. No public building is complete without its intrusive clock face, no wrist so small that it cannot have strapped to it an expression of the passing of time. And in case we fail to give due deference to the passage of time, we are reminded by alarms—strident, loud, or a tinkling tune—all saying, 'You must do it, have it, experience it, *now*, for time is passing.'

Jesus took his time, because he waited for the right time in God's economy. He took time to listen to God, while he got on with what needed doing. During the two days of waiting, he would discover what was to come. The way to glory was open, and that way was through death to life.

When Jesus made his decision and told his disciples, they tried to dissuade him. They knew that it spelled danger. When he asked them to go with him, I imagine there were murmurings, fear for their own skins; for they knew it was likely that whatever would befall Jesus would be their fate also. Thomas, the one we malign as the doubter, faced up to the fact of the situation, and took the lead with courage: 'Let us go... so that we may die with him!' Thomas was prepared to give everything, even life itself, to be with Jesus.

Was he scared? Did he really realize how desperate the situation was? I believe he was and did, for Thomas was a down-to-earth facer of facts; and so his courage was even greater, for he knew the odds and accepted them. What really mattered was being with Jesus; that outweighed comfort or safety.

None of us likes putting our head into a noose. Most of us would choose a life of calm, secure contentment. Oh yes, we want to be stimulated, excited, enriched by life—but within safe bounds. Our life is very precious. It is to be guarded, for we have only the one life and therefore we must make the most of it and use it to its full extent. We all have an inbuilt defence mechanism, a self-preservation instinct. And yet in certain circumstances something or someone else can transcend those restrictions. We can 'live dangerously'. It will be because of love—love for a child, for friend, for country; that love which Jesus describes as totally self-giving. The fear of death can be outweighed by the power of love, and the fact of death freely accepted as the cost of living.

There is no barrier that can withstand love. That fact Jesus and his friends were now on their way to prove for all time.

# CHAPTER 2

# 'Too late, too late,' was the cry

## JOHN 11:17–37

When death or tragedy occurs, life for those closest—the family, friends—goes into reverse. Each moment, each event, is analysed, almost as though by doing so we can reverse the irreversible. The words I hear most frequently as I visit a bereaved family are 'If only...' I can see in their faces the sorrow because of what might have been. Death has come down like a curtain, blotting out the signs of the future. There seems only one way to look, and that is back. It is then that the past comes tumbling back, with its missed opportunities and wrong turnings. It is then that blame is apportioned, guilt rises, accusations are made.

I have sat in homes where, although not a word has been spoken, I have felt the atmosphere of regret, guilt and accusations. These are natural reactions, although people often are ashamed to feel them, and so keep them bottled up; but they are much better brought out into the open and expressed, so that they can be dealt with rather than allowed to become festering wounds and a blight on the future.

Martha and Mary sent the message to Jesus that his friend, their brother Lazarus, was ill. They confidently expected that he would help them, and that their brother would recover. What did they feel as they saw Lazarus grow steadily worse, until the battle for life was lost? Then there followed the elaborate ceremonies, the burial and the mourning, all according to custom. Friends and neighbours came to share this time, to pay their respects and to be with the sisters—but no Jesus.

At last, four days after the funeral, Jesus appeared—too late, much too late. Too late to help Lazarus, too late to be at the burial, too late to be of any assistance. The one person the sisters had wanted to be there was too late. How did they feel when they heard that Jesus was almost at the door? Martha went out to meet him; Mary stayed in the house. Did she stay in because she could not bring herself to face Jesus, to speak of her brother's death? Was she disappointed in him? Was she angry with him? How many times did she say and think, 'If only...'?

Martha met Jesus with those words: 'If you had been here, Lord, my brother would not have died.' She believed in her Lord who healed the sick; but could she believe in a Lord who raised the dead? She believed that Jesus was in a special relationship with God, and so the impossible was possible; but how that was to be, she did not know. She could only cry out with faith in the orthodox Jewish belief in life after death, unknown and shadowy, but real: 'I know that he will rise to life on the last day.'

Martha's faith was like the mustard seed, so small and simple, yet containing the germ of life and potential for growth. Jesus responded with those words which still bring comfort and hope to mourners in a present-day city crematorium, with its canned hymns and plastic flowers, as much as to that grieving country girl who stood before him: 'I am the resurrection and the life.' That girl could only look into his eyes and answer with confidence his question, 'Do you believe this?' for she knew him as a friend. She knew him personally; she knew, too, that he was the Messiah, the Son of God, the one for whom her people the Jews had looked for all those centuries.

I look into the faces of the mourners when I take a funeral. Sometimes the church is crowded with friends and relations, there to pay their last respects. There are times when, by the graveside at the funeral of an elderly person, there may be just one surviving relative. Or, when the death has been sudden, or of a young person, the church or crematorium is filled with young people, who perhaps had never given death a thought until a road crash or disease, raging like a forest fire, had snatched the life of one of their friends. I see grief, despair, fear, anger. They look at me, searching for an answer, hoping for some light; and whatever the circumstances, I can look back at them and say, 'Jesus says: "I am the resurrection and the life."'

Do they believe me? Some do, some don't. Their faces give me their answer. Sometimes I realize that they pity me for believing the words I say. But often I see the answer, 'I do believe', and I know that they will be able to cope, to come to terms with death, because they know that death is not the end, because they trust in the promise of Jesus. They have something to hold on to, a future to look forward to.

Martha knew that assurance in her grief, and her first thought was to share it with her sister, Mary. But she knew that Mary would want to hear it from Jesus himself, and so she lovingly took the initiative and gave her sister the message that Jesus wanted to see her. She wanted Mary to have time with him alone so that he could give her the comfort and assurance she needed, to face what was to come.

In our anxiety to help the bereaved, we talk too much. It is a natural reaction: we think we are helping them by not allowing them to be alone, to brood, to cry, to remember. The bereaved are given sleeping pills to 'get them through the night', to keep them from thinking about what has happened. And yet what they do need is time—time when they can unburden their hearts before God, time to question him, to be angry, to cry, to complain, and to allow him to meet with them.

When I visit the bereaved, I just listen to them, allow them to tell me all that they want to say, and then I give them space. I leave a card which has verses from scripture, such as Jesus' words, 'I am the resurrection and the life', and one or two simple prayers. I say, 'Tell him how you feel. Let him bring you his comfort. Give him a chance to meet you in your need'... and I go back the next day when they have had a chance to be alone.

There are many times when, as I leave the bereaved person and get into my car, I weep for them; especially when they are friends, people I know, members of our church. It is impossible to be detached, to be unaffected; and Jesus himself was affected deeply by the death of his friend and the grief of the bereaved sisters. Perhaps one of the most poignant verses in the Bible is the short-est verse of all, 'Jesus wept'. In those two words we have the pic-ture of his identification with human suffering. In those two words lies the answer to those who say, 'Why doesn't God do some-thing?' Here we have our assurance of his concern, his love.

The God who weeps—yet he was misunderstood then, as now. Some saw love, others saw indifference. It is the same today as we look out on the suffering world, and see across it the shadow of the cross. Some see in that cross the love of God, the self-giving God; for others it is the sign of failure and of defeat.

Death comes to us all. It can come at any time. Some fight it long and hard; others wait for it, indeed would welcome it. Often it is unexpected; a split second separates life from death. The great and famous have their death reported in *The Times*, and splendid services are held. Those who meet their death through violence often have attending TV cameras, and the funeral may be the grounds for demonstration and further violence. But most deaths pass unnoticed, except by a few. The local paper carries a brief announcement, the shoppers barely glance at the hearse going slowly along the high street on the way to the municipal cemetery or crematorium.

Death is inevitable. It is the one sure fact of life. From the moment we come into the world, we are on our way out of it. Death catches up with us all in the end. Death is the last word—or is it?

What of the one who says, 'I am the resurrection and the life'? How can anyone claim to be that? Who does he think he is—God?

# CHAPTER 3

# Moment of truth

## JOHN 11:38-54

Blondin was the most famous acrobat of all time; he performed the seemingly impossible by crossing the Niagara Falls on a tightrope. The crowd held their breath as he did what had never been done before—the most death-defying performance ever witnessed.

When he reached the other side, he asked the crowd whether they believed he could do it again. Yes, they believed he could! But what about if he was blindfolded, *and* wheeled a barrow across, *and* twirled an umbrella at the same time? Oh yes, they believed he could! And what if he carried a man on his back? Who believed he could do that as well? Many expressed their confidence. Then he asked for a volunteer—that was a different story!

How many of those who said they believed he could do it would have taken up his challenge, even after seeing him cross once? Many believed he could do it, but very few would have put their faith to the test. Would you? I often wonder who had to have the greater faith, Blondin or the man on his back. I suppose the difference was that Blondin had faith in himself, while the man on his back had to put his faith in Blondin; he was totally dependent on Blondin to get him across, and could do nothing but trust him.

As Jesus went to the grave of his friend Lazarus, what did Martha and Mary and the people who were with them think he was going to do? To pay his respects? To weep? Martha and Mary had both affirmed their belief that Jesus could have prevented the death of their brother, *if* he had arrived in time. Martha had declared her faith in Jesus as the Son of God, the one who could bring life out of death. How did she feel as Jesus approached her brother's tomb?

Then Jesus spoke. 'Take away the stone,' he ordered. You can almost hear the intake of breath as he said those words. Silence descended; no one moved. Then Martha, in a down-to-earth statement, voiced what they were all thinking, what they all feared to experience. 'There will be a bad smell, Lord. He has been buried four days!' The Authorized Version of the Bible puts it even more strongly: 'Lord, by this time he stinketh.' Martha was right. Four days dead in a hot climate, the smell and the sight would be terrible indeed. Anyone who has lived in such a climate knows only too well that burial must follow death as quickly as possible for that reason. Decay sets in swiftly; the body must be removed immediately.

Jesus reminded Martha of what he had told her, and what she had affirmed; there was no more protest. The stone was moved out of position, the seal was broken, and Jesus gave thanks to his Father in heaven for listening to him, thanking his Father that the people would see God's glory. In doing so, he testified to the power of God the Father, staking his all on his Father's action. He gave a visual aid to the power of prayer so that the people might know that God answers prayer, that God is the giver of life, that God has power over death itself. Jesus raised his eyes to heaven. He raised the eyes of those who stood with him at the graveside, to heaven, to God. Jesus gave his Father all the glory.

Then came the word of command: 'Lazarus, come out!' And out of the grave came no bad smell, but the living man Lazarus. Imagine the sight—the man walking out of the grave, from death into life, covered with the clothing of the dead. It must have been an awesome sight. Some may have thought it was a ghost or a vision. The trappings of death were removed; they were not needed. Lazarus was alive and well. He had not only been brought back to life, but back from the process of decay. He stood before them, the evidence and proof of the power of God, the testament to God's glory. There could be no argument. He had died. He had been buried. He should have been a stinking corpse. No way could anyone explain it away. The moment of truth was there before their very eyes.

What more did anyone need to believe Jesus? What more could they ask? For many it was enough, but that did not mean that they all wanted to follow Jesus. Quite the opposite! A council meeting of religious leaders was called. Whether Jesus had really raised Lazarus was not disputed—how could it be? But the purpose of their meeting was not to rejoice with Lazarus, or to give God the glory, or to accept Jesus as the one whom God had sent to them.

It was to decide how to get rid of Jesus. They could not allow him to go around raising people from the dead—that was dangerous; it could mean trouble. They could put up with the preaching, tolerate some of his healings—those could always be explained away if they worked hard enough at it—but raising people from the dead was too much. Jesus would have to go. He was a trouble-maker, a danger to the lives, comfort and status of the religious leaders.

Jesus is still a danger, and for the same reason. He brings the dead to life. For that reason, Christians, those who follow Jesus, are seen as dangerous even today in many parts of the world. Councils pronounce sentence on them. They are too dangerous to be allowed to live.

If Jesus had been just a teacher, one who taught a way of life that was of a moral, caring, serving system; if he had just preached a gospel of love and peace; then he could have been accepted quite happily. It would have been acceptable to have had a few people healed—after all, these things do happen from time to time, for various reasons. Even the medical profession acknowledges that sometimes symptoms disappear on their own, illnesses clear up, and there is the mystery of long-term remission. If people have faith that something is helping, then maybe it can; we have all heard of the coloured water that is believed to be medicine and therefore seems to do the trick—it's all in the mind, there is a perfectly logical explanation.

A teaching, preaching, even healing Jesus can be tolerated in any society. He can take his place alongside all the other so-called 'gods' to be nodded at now and again and used to grace ceremonial occasions—he cannot do any harm, and there is always a possibility that he may do a little good, if you like that sort of thing. If, however, he is the Son of God; if he has brought others to life; if he is alive and active in the world; then he is dangerous. He cannot be allowed to go free, and neither can those who claim to belong to him, who say they have authority to continue his work in his way and in his power.

What sort of Jesus do we believe in, I wonder? Do we believe he has raised the dead to life? Did he actually bring to life a man who had been dead for four days, or is it just a story, an illustration of a spiritual truth, or even perhaps a gross exaggeration? It is hard to accept for sophisticated men and women in our technological age, when even some leaders in his Church explain away such events, write learned books on the subject, and tell us that 'in the light of experience' it could not have happened and therefore did not happen.

Perhaps the majority of those who watched Blondin cross the gap between earth and sky believed he could do it again; they would raise their hands and give him their vote of confidence. They had faith in him; but the test of their faith was whether they were personally willing to be carried by him across the gap. Jesus was the one person who, in modern language, had the faith to 'put his money where his mouth was', and risk everything, even life itself. In return he shared the triumph and the glory.

It reminds me of the saying, 'If he is not Lord of all, he is not Lord at all.' Faith means staking everything on Jesus Christ, allowing him to carry us across the gap—and with no safety net either!

Did he raise the dead, or didn't he? Could he? Can he? Will he? Dare we risk the stone being rolled away from the tomb that holds our own fears, our own death and decay? What if all that comes out is a bad smell? ... But then that is the risk we must take, if we really want to know.

# CHAPTER 4

# Home for the feast

## JOHN 11:55–57

To go home for Christmas is the hope of most people, whatever their age. They may have spread their wings and gone off to distant places to live and work; they may have families of their own, and have settled into a new community; but as Christmas time approaches, all thoughts go to 'home'. Where their parents live, where the family home is, there they belong.

When Christmas week arrives, our airports, railway stations and bus depots are crowded with folk, heavily laden with cases and parcels, 'going home'. Travelling at Christmas time is quite different from normal. People talk to each other, they smile, exchange confidences—and some even sing on the way! For those not able to get home, messages via the post, telephone, e-mail or 'Interflora' span the miles, as the next best thing to being with loved ones at the festive season. The radio stations are inundated with requests for a mention, and promises are made over the air: 'Sorry I can't make it this year, but hope to see you next Christmas.'

At the other end, preparations are being made to receive the family members coming home: rooms are prepared, favourite dishes cooked, the decorations and trees with shining lights say, 'Welcome home!' Then comes the joy of reunion as the plane touches down, the train pulls in, coaches arrive, the car turns into the drive. There are hugs and kisses, laughter and tears, the family is complete; they are all home for Christmas.

The Feast of the Passover in Jesus' time wasn't quite like our Christmas. It was far more a religious obligation than a family celebration, but they have much in common. Everyone wanted to be home for Passover, and 'home' for every Jew was—as it still is—Jerusalem. It was obligatory for every male Jew who lived within fifteen miles of Jerusalem to get there, regardless of the inconvenience, but they would come from much further afield. It was seen not just as a duty but as a joy.

The roads to Jerusalem would be a continuous stream of people. No planes, coaches or cars—they walked! And so the roads were put into good order, the bridges repaired, ready for the pilgrims who were on their way home for the feast from far and wide. For the pilgrims themselves, there would be eager exchanges of news, plenty of gossip and speculation, and there would be the singing of psalms, rejoicing in God and his greatness, psalms of deliverance, psalms of victory.

There was one big problem, though, which overshadowed all else. The Jewish people were under an army of occupation. They may have been in their own homeland, but they were subject to their occupying power, that of Rome. This was always resented and hated—the fact that, although they had been delivered by God out of Egypt all those years ago, they were now once more in captivity. In their longing to be free, they looked for a deliverer, a saviour. And at Passover time especially, nationalistic feelings ran high, fanning the flames of bitterness and resentment, so that the crowds of pilgrims on their way to Jerusalem were not exactly happy, carefree travellers. Excited, yes. Full of purpose and idealism, yes. Delighted to be with their fellows, yes. But, oh that circumstances were different! They longed to be free as they advanced upon their beloved Jerusalem.

For the Romans, Passover time was one big headache, a time to be on 'full alert'. It was never easy, being the occupying army. There was no love lost between the Jews and the Romans. The rule of the sword, the fear of the lash, the shadow of the cross, kept the Jews in submission; but the Romans knew that at any time there could be an uprising of these fanatically nationalistic people. The only authority the Jews took notice of was their religious leaders, so the Romans knew it was as well to cultivate these, giving them some concessions in return for using their influence to keep under control the more passionate nationalists.

This Passover there was another complication—Jesus of Nazareth. There were many rumours flying around about him. He had achieved a large following, mostly amongst the ordinary folk, with his teaching and preaching and reported healings. He had got rather too popular. Some were even saying he was the Saviour, the promised deliverer sent from God. If reports were to be believed, he had even raised a man from the dead! So he could prove very dangerous indeed. He had not been greeted favourably or with acclaim by the religious leaders of his people. Oh yes, there were some who were important who secretly agreed with him—but he was too 'way out'. He didn't conform to the accepted patterns. He could cause real trouble for those who had settled into an uneasy truce with the Romans, those who chose peace at any price.

The Romans did not want any more trouble. They had enough on their hands already, with so many people on the move for Passover, and there was always the danger of riots and confrontation. They hoped the Jewish authorities would sort this Jesus out between themselves. It would be easier and cleaner if they did. If it was a religious argument, then let the religious leaders deal with it. All the Romans wanted was for Passover to pass over as quietly and as peaceably as possible, then to get back to normal routine.

The chief priests and Pharisees didn't want Jesus around at the Passover, for there was always the possibility that the crowds might find in him what they were looking for. They might get ideas about making him a king or a ruler, ousting the present religious authorities. And so orders were given that anyone who knew where Jesus was should disclose it, so that he might be 'attended to' and taken into custody before he could influence any more people.

Jesus, quite aware of their plans, quietly went with his friends to Ephraim, north of Jerusalem, 'out in the sticks'. There he was safe, away from the main stream, away from those who for various reasons wanted to dispose of him.

For the pilgrims going up to Jerusalem, Jesus was the main topic of conversation. Many had stories to tell of hearing and seeing him. He was the focus of speculation. The crowds were not stupid; they knew what was going on, the plans that were being made to get rid of him. They knew, too, that he was a most extraordinary person. It was impossible to be neutral about him. He demanded a response. So, on the road to Jerusalem, views for and against would be fiercely expressed, and the big question was, 'Will Jesus come for the feast?' Some said, 'If he knows what's good for him, he will keep away. He would be a fool to come; he would walk straight into trouble.' Yet others, knowing that Jesus was a religious Jew, who always observed the festivals, felt sure that he would come. He would perform his obligation, whether it meant his arrest or not. There were those who hoped that if and when he came, it would be the big showdown between the Jews and the Romans—Jesus would lead them to victory, God would enable him to destroy the occupying powers; this Passover could be a time of rejoicing and triumph.

Just a few days to go! Excitement was at fever pitch, Jerusalem was getting even more crowded, people were on the move, everything was coming to a head... And Jesus, where was he now? He too was on the move, to visit friends, to enjoy a meal with some very special friends indeed—Mary, Martha and the one who came back from the dead, Lazarus, their brother. It was to be a party with a difference, in more ways than one; for, though they did not know it, it would be the last opportunity he would have to be with those friends, the last opportunity for them to show him how much they loved him. And what happened was recorded for all time, for us too to ponder over, to consider our verdict over love's extravagance.

CHAPTER 5

# *A celebration dinner*

## JOHN 12:1–11

Sitting over lunch in the canteen after a hard morning's work recording programmes, when I was the Anglican Religious Adviser at Yorkshire Television, two of us were chatting away about all sorts of subjects, including the weather, the government and the fortunes, or otherwise, of Leeds United. Then suddenly, out of the blue, my companion said, 'If Lazarus came back from the dead, why aren't we told what he said when he came back? He surely must have said something!'

I must admit the question threw me, because it's true—we have a record of the raising of Lazarus, and he is mentioned several times, but we hear nothing from his own mouth. We have a very full description of the scene, of the conversation between the sisters, Martha and Mary, and Jesus, but from Lazarus—nothing.

My immediate answer was that the Gospels don't record everything happening in the ministry of Jesus, or every conversation—they give a condensed picture—but what we have gives us sufficient to grasp who Jesus was, and how he lived here on earth. We have the outstanding situations, examples of his attitudes towards all sorts of people, the highlights of his teaching, preaching and healing ministry. The Gospels are rather like a family photograph album, with a series of snapshots, rather than a diary. I quoted to my friend some words from near the end of John's Gospel: 'In his disciples' presence Jesus performed many other miracles which are not written down in this book. But these have been written in order that you may believe that Jesus is the Messiah, the Son of God, and that through your faith in him you may have life' (John 20:30–31).

My questioner, although obviously impressed with my ability to quote chapter and verse, was still not satisfied. He protested. 'But it would help people like me to believe if we could read the account of dying and coming back by the person it happened to.'

I can understand my questioner. It would have been helpful to have been able to read the actual words Lazarus spoke. But it is quite clear that he did die, and that he came back from the dead, and was still around some time later, alive and well and enjoying a meal at home with his family. In fact, his sisters Martha and Mary prepared a special celebration dinner for their friends, and Jesus was the guest of honour at it. Martha, true to form, helped to serve the meal. We can imagine her busy, fussing, happy to do what she loved doing, giving pleasure to family and friends by putting on a good spread. It was her way of saying thank you to Jesus, showing her love for him in a practical way.

There is a retreat house in Yorkshire, run by the Sisters of the Order of the Holy Paraclete. It is just a couple of miles away from Whitby, tucked away from the main road amid the most glorious countryside. When I was there on retreat, one of the things that impressed me was the obvious joy the sisters found in serving their guests; the pleasure on their faces as they dished up the meals or poured out the coffee. I can see now one of the sisters cleaning the windows with an expression of blissful happiness. I saw it in the way they all worked together, in the extra little touches such as flowers in the bedrooms, how the meals were arranged and the shine on the furniture. That service was, for them, part of their joyful commitment to God; nothing was too much because it was a labour of love. I owe a lot to the loving Marthas of the Order of the Holy Paraclete at Sleights!

I think too of those in our parish who delight to serve in the very mundane practical things like cleaning the church, repairing the woodwork, tidying the surrounding gardens, keeping the linen in good repair—all labours of love. If I asked those people to get up and preach a sermon, to teach in Sunday school or even to read a lesson, they would run a mile; and yet they equally serve their Lord in the generous and unstinted way they give of themselves in the down-to-earth practical things. We thank God for all the Marthas!

And what about Mary? We read that 'they' prepared a dinner. I like to think that Mary had done her fair share in the preparation, but now lets her sister bask in the glory of being the hostess—not to get out of helping to serve, but to let her sister have the honour of being in charge of the celebrations. The food was the very best they could provide; nothing was too good for the Master, the one who had given them back their brother from the dead, the one who they knew would give them all eternal life beyond the grave.

Mary, full of love, also gave of her best to Jesus. She gave the most precious thing she possessed, an expensive perfume which represented her life's savings. She didn't hand it to him, she humbly poured it over his feet, and then, as an act of loving abandonment, wiped his feet with her hair.

What did the guests think of her action? I imagine some would have been embarrassed at such an emotional exhibition, others puzzled, surprised, impressed by the magnitude of the gift and the expression of it. When I read the account I can almost smell that perfume. John says, 'The sweet smell of the perfume filled the whole house'—and that sweet smell of love's extravagance fills the room where I, two thousand years later, recall that moment. It is one of the most beautiful acts of love ever recorded in history. It is the supreme example of the response of a loving heart.

Yet when it happened, one man was very annoyed indeed. He could see only the monetary value of the perfume. To him it was sheer waste. He did not see or smell love; it left a sour taste in his mouth. He was angry with the giver—she must be mad! What a waste! If she had wanted to give away the perfume, why hadn't she sold it so that the money could have been used to give practical help to poor people?

He had a point, hadn't he? After all, he was the one who looked after the cash side of things, the one who had to pay the bills. He had been entrusted by Jesus and the others to take charge of the finances. He could have done so much more with that perfume, or with the realized value of it—and now it was wasted! All that was left was the smell, and soon that would evaporate.

How wrong he was! That sweet smell of love has never evaporated. It has filled the whole world, and has prompted others to give their all in thanksgiving for what Jesus has done for them in their lives.

The Gospel account tells us that the man who objected was the one who soon would betray Jesus for just one tenth of the value of that perfume—Judas Iscariot. We are told he was a thief, who betrayed the confidence that had been put in him. I still wonder, though, whether he actually stole the money for himself, or whether it was just that he saw everything in cash terms, since he was the elected treasurer. It may be that he saw the Kingdom of God only in terms of an earthly kingdom, which would inevitably need cash support. He may have been a very efficient steward of the group's resources. I don't know, I can't judge. All I can do is feel very sorry for him that he missed out on the joy because he was only bothered about the tinkle of coins. He could not smell the sweetness because of his own acidity of life.

There are still those today who see the Kingdom of God in terms of money. Their commitment to Christ is in relation to the smallest coin in their pocket. I have been in churches when we have all sung the hymn 'Take my life, and let it be consecrated, Lord, to thee' with great vigour, and the words 'Take my silver and my gold, not a mite would I withhold' with rousing enthusiasm—and then I have received the offertory plate and seen small change only! It has been said that the last part of a man to be converted is his pocket. Books are written, sermons preached, campaigns arranged, to encourage the faithful to give to the Lord, and very few respond with more than a token amount.

It is not only with our money that we are mean, of course. How stinting we are with our offering of ourselves, our time, our abilities, our love! For most of us, these are things we measure out carefully, rather than pour out generously. Why did Mary give her all, and so emotionally? Wasn't it because she knew and appreciated what Jesus had done for her?

Mary did what she knew she had to do when she poured out her fragrant offering over the feet of her Lord—she responded to the opportunity she had to show her love. That special moment would never come again; she took it when it came, oblivious to what others thought of her action. How many times are we prompted within to do some act of kindness, take a certain course of action, make a generous gesture—and then have second thoughts? What will others think of us? Is it the most sensible thing to do? Wouldn't it be better to wait until later? So we hesitate, and we are lost, because the time has gone; we had our opportunity and we did not rise to it.

I remember some words written in my autograph book many years ago: 'I expect to pass through this world but once; any good thing therefore that I can do, or any kindness that I can show to any fellow creature, let me do it now; let me not defer nor neglect it, for I shall not pass this way again.'

So we have Martha, whose joy it was to serve, and Mary, whose delight it was to give. And what of Lazarus? He was the living witness at the celebration. He spoke by his very presence. The people gathered to see Jesus, who had raised a man from the dead, and Lazarus, who was that man. Here was the evidence people looked for, the evidence that tipped the scales in favour of Jesus. And yet, while many people rejoiced, others were plotting to wipe out the evidence. Lazarus, too, must be destroyed; for while he lived, that man who came back from the dead would attract men and women to follow Jesus.

When we become Christians we come out of death into life. We are the living witnesses, to be seen in our homes, at work, in the community, as well as in our church activities. Do those who meet us know we are different? What effect do we have on them? If we are true witnesses, then we will have the same effect as Lazarus. We will be the living proof of Jesus Christ, and some will come to believe in him: but others will hate us and they will seek to remove us. As Christians, we have to be willing to accept the consequences, for his sake, whatever that may mean.

# CHAPTER 6

# *The victory parade*

## JOHN 12:12–22

I grew up in a small Cheshire town. We lived a couple of miles from the town centre, and I remember that as a child it was quite an adventure to go 'down into town'. It was a very ordinary sort of place, with not a great deal of excitement, so when there was a special event everybody turned out for it. One of the events I remember very vividly was the homecoming of a local soldier who had won the Victoria Cross during the war.

He was a very ordinary chap, by all accounts. Some people shook their heads and said he was a bit of a tearaway; others said that going into the army had been the making of him. Anyway, he had shown great bravery and was awarded the VC, and had been promoted to sergeant, and it was decided to have a 'Welcome Home' for him in the town. I stood with my friends and enthusiastically waved my Union Jack, and everybody cheered. The cheering got louder and louder, and folk were jumping up and down, and then came the sound of the band, and we could see, standing up on a lorry, some of the local dignitaries—and with them the smiling, khaki-clad figure of our VC. I can recall him now; he looked so big and handsome, with his sergeant's stripes on his arms, and the shining medal on his chest for all to see. We all went hoarse with shouting and cheering. It was a marvellous day.

Some years later I saw him in the town. In ordinary clothes and without all the trappings of uniform and medal, he looked very insignificant, much smaller than he had seemed standing on the lorry. Looking back, I suppose it was all the excitement of the day, the cheering, the bunting, the being part of an exuberant crowd, that had made it all so thrilling. I had been carried along with the crowd, caught up in the magic of it all.

Whenever I read the account of Jesus coming into Jerusalem on the first Palm Sunday, I always remember that victory parade in Congleton, Cheshire, with all of us waiting for the hero to come,

31

and making sure he got a great reception. Jesus came into Jerusalem as a hero too—after all, he had fed the hungry, healed the sick, raised the dead; there was nothing he could not do. The ordinary people, who had been downtrodden for so long under Roman oppression, who looked for the King, the Messiah promised by God, at last had real hope. They could see their King. He was here at last. For them it was not only a political occasion but a spiritual one, for the Messiah was God's anointed. Nothing, and no one, would be able to stand against him; and the people would share in his victory. No wonder they cheered. No wonder they waved the palms. No wonder they shouted, 'Praise God!'

And Jesus the King came... on a donkey. It really was ridiculous, a king on a donkey! Imagine the Queen going on a royal tour in a Robin Reliant or a battered old Mini—it would destroy the dignity of the occasion, make nonsense of a royal celebration and be seen as an insult to her hosts.

So why a donkey? Those people who understood the scriptures would know that it was by no accident, but in direct fulfilment of the words of the prophet Zechariah:

> *Rejoice, rejoice, people of Zion!*
> *Shout for joy, you people of Jerusalem!*
> *Look, your king is coming to you!*
> *He comes triumphant and victorious,*
> *but humble and riding on a donkey—*
> *on a colt, the foal of a donkey.*

**Zechariah 9:9**

Maybe some in the crowd remembered this prophecy and knew that this was the promised one who would deliver them, but even they would fail to grasp what sort of a victory it was to be. Later on they would shake their heads sadly and say, 'We had hoped he would be the one who would have set Israel free!' (Luke 24:21). Gradually for some, dramatically for others, the truth would sink in. They would realize that the King did indeed enter Jerusalem on that day, and that his Kingdom has no end.

On the day, though, all the crowd could think was, 'Freedom at last! Victory is ours. Jesus is king.' Life from now on would be altogether different—they would be free for ever.

Yes, they were right! Jesus would free them from sin, from death, for he was the one who raised men from the dead. He was the giver of life; but not quite as they had imagined. His new lifestyle was not the gift of an earthly king to his loyal subjects, but the gift of eternal life for all who would trust him as Saviour and as Lord.

And the cheers went on and on, and the crowd got bigger and more excited, and the praise and adulation rang stronger. The Pharisees were in deep trouble. They sensed they were in danger of defeat; they were losing out to Jesus. He was the hero of the day. 'Look, the whole world is following him!' they commented bitterly, and they were right. Jesus had captured the hearts of all in the city. Even the foreigners were following him. The world had gathered in Jerusalem. The world had glimpsed the glory of God in the man on the donkey.

The Pharisees were powerless—for a time. Soon, though, they would gather their forces and throw everything into destroying Jesus. They would even seem to succeed. They would nail him down—that would silence the crowd; after all, what use is a dead hero?

Two thousand years have gone by since the King rode in on a donkey. He is still riding in, humbly, yet regally, into men's and women's hearts and lives. The world still goes after him, and nothing can stop him.

The world came to Jerusalem. Many came to worship—not only Jews, but those who were seekers after God, who wanted to know and understand the things of God; the religious, the curious, the pious and the puzzled.

There were also those who came along to see the show, to 'watch the world go by'. Among them were some Greeks, who were there for the festival. Jesus interested them, and they wanted to meet him, so they approached Philip. Why Philip? Maybe his Greek name gave them the confidence to approach him—or his friendly nature. He could have been pointed out as someone who would introduce them to Jesus, or then again it might have been that he saw they were wanting help and offered it. Who knows? Anyway, Philip told Andrew, and together they approached Jesus, for they knew he would turn no one away.

And so it is, still. But whoever does come to Jesus will be left with no false illusions as to what following him means. It means handing over everything. It is total commitment, even to death. It means risking all you have, and in exchange—life and glory! The terms and conditions of service are plainly laid out. Jesus makes sure that those who wish to follow him know the cost—and the reward. Whether they take up his offer or not is entirely up to each individual.

Many today say wistfully, 'We would like to see Jesus.' They are outsiders, standing on the edge and watching what is going on in the Christian Church. They see the trappings of faith. They hear the arguments, read the reports, witness the ceremonies. Something within them stirs, questions, responds; but they need to be able to get to the heart of what it's all about. They need to see Jesus for themselves.

I talk to all sorts of people, and I find that many who do not claim to be Christians, and who never come to church, are still fascinated with Jesus. They want to know more, but who can they ask? Who dare they approach? I discover that many have tried to enquire, but have met with a blank wall. Some have ventured into churches and have not been made welcome, so have not tried again. Sadly, I have to admit that this is often true. We have our cosy church 'clubs', our own circle of Christian friends who are like ourselves, who we feel easy with. We do not take kindly to outsiders—especially if they are different, if they don't speak our language or don't know the rules.

The glory of Jesus is that he is for the world—for everyone. It was so hard for people to understand that when he was here on earth. His friends wanted to keep him for their exclusive use—after all, he was a Jew; he had come 'to fulfil the law and the prophets'; he was 'King of the Jews'. One of the biggest problems of the Church after Pentecost was to realize that Gentiles did not have to become Jews before they could be accepted by Jesus; they were accepted as themselves. And what about the position of women? Jesus afforded to women the same privileges as men; they could be his friends, they were equally valued and loved. But even today the Church struggles with the position of women, often relegating them to the menial tasks, refusing them the joy of serving their Lord as ministers, pastors or teachers.

It was to the Pharisee Nicodemus that Jesus spoke the words of invitation, available for all (the story is in chapter 3 of John's

Gospel): 'The Son of man must be lifted up, so that everyone who believes in him may have eternal life. For God loved the world so much that he gave his only Son, so that everyone who believes in him may not die but have eternal life.' That promise was for the Pharisees and for the dying thief crucified with Jesus, for the Roman soldiers who hammered in the nails, for the persecutor of Christians, Saul, later called Paul. It was for the small known world of yesterday, and for the citizens of today's 'global village'—for all races, colours, cultures. For the gifted undergraduate, the child who will never progress beyond the mental age of a baby, the titled owner of the stately home and the one who resides in Her Majesty's Prison.

When Jesus saw the Greeks coming to meet him, he knew that the glory of the Father was being revealed, that the time was almost at hand when he would be literally 'lifted up' before the whole world. That glory meant death on the cross, before the glory of heaven.

So what difference does it make to me? I know all this. I know that Jesus died for the world—for the good, the bad and the very indifferent. Yet I have to ask myself: do I share him with the world, my world? What have I got to say to the person who wastes my time, makes impossible demands upon me, uses me? Do I show them the glory of the Lord, or am I hiding it from them? Who do I include in my world? I must confess that my world is mainly the people I choose to be part of it. What conceit! It is not my world at all, it is God's world. I am part of his world. I am loved and wanted and so are all the rest.

So, although I may not like it, I am forced to accept the value of every other person, whoever and whatever they are—and Jesus wants them to meet him and to get to know him. So what am I to answer when the request comes, 'We would like to see Jesus'? Is there anything in me that will prompt that request? I wonder. I do indeed wonder.

# CHAPTER 7

# Which way to glory?

## JOHN 12:23–50

*No pain, no palm; No thorns, no throne;*
*No gall, no glory; No cross, no crown.*

The words are by William Penn (1644–1718), the English Quaker who founded the American colony of Pennsylvania. In his stark alternatives we see the choice that faces all of us. If only there was a way round, a diversion we could take that would avoid the pain, the thorns, the gall and the cross! If only we could slip off the road and rejoin it later, having avoided the uneven surface and the pitted track, so that we would just have to coast down the final straight! If God is God, we tell ourselves, if he loves and cares for us, if he rules supreme over earth and heaven, then surely he would point out a diversion to us, wave us through and meet us at the other end, having cleared all obstacles away and given us an easy passage.

Jesus must have felt just like this. He did not look forward to suffering, to having his life ended so horribly and brutally. He did not like the look of the journey ahead. He was still a young man, at the height of his strength and powers. Life apparently lay ahead, full of endless possibilities. He had just begun to make real headway; at last his message was beginning to get through, not only to his friends and his own people, but to the world. The horizon was widening; the sky was the limit. His prayer was that glory might be brought to his Father's name, and his Father had spoken those words of assurance: 'I have brought glory to it, and I will do so again!'

Over and over again, Jesus had brought glory to his Father, in his birth, in his baptism, through his ministry. But there was no short cut to the final glory. Jesus knew he would be lifted up before all the world, present and to come—but at what cost to himself!

The voice of his Father assured him of the glory; but more than that, it was to assure the world that what was to come was the culmination of God's glorious plan for all humanity. It was not a horrible disaster or mistake, but the way of final triumph.

The crowd heard something, but did not recognize the voice of God. They knew something had happened. Some explained it away naturally—'it thundered'. Others felt it was more than a coincidence; it was an angel talking to Jesus, but not to them. They did not hear the voice of divine approval. If they had done, then maybe they would have taken notice of the one who stood before them.

If the crowd had known how short a time they would have Jesus with them, maybe they would have listened to him. Maybe they would have let go of their own ideas, and been willing to let him shed light on the things that confused them, that they didn't understand, and that didn't seem to make sense. Jesus made one last appeal to them, offering them the light they needed. They had seen him give sight to the blind. He had proved he was a giver of the light. He had stood before them and declared, 'I am the light of the world.' He had offered them the light of life; but for the most part they didn't want to see or know.

What more could he do? He had offered them everything, proved his words by his deeds, and still they did not believe in him. It seemed impossible, and yet it was true. So Jesus left them, and went away. John records the words of the prophet Isaiah:

> *Lord, who believed the message we told?*
> *To whom did the Lord reveal his power?*

*And so they were not able to believe, because Isaiah also said:*

> *God has blinded their eyes*
> *and closed their minds,*
> *so that their eyes would not see,*
> *and their minds would not understand,*
> *and they would not turn to me, says God,*
> *for me to heal them.*

Isaiah had prophesied that when the Messiah came he would not be accepted. People would be blind to him because they were so sure they knew what God would do and how he would act. They had become hardened, and so they were unable to see God at work right there in their midst. It was tragic when you think about it. Jesus was with them, right there—they saw him, witnessed him at work, heard his words—and yet they did not see, did not want to see. It seems beyond belief.

Beyond belief! Is he beyond belief today, even though we can see him at work, and hear his words? Or are we still too tied up in arguments, blindly yet cleverly using words of scripture for our own purposes? 'You can make the Bible prove anything you want it to'—how often I have heard that! Shame on us, that we take the Word of God and use it to suit ourselves. We pick and choose, dismiss the parts we do not like or understand, and finish up with a pretty package that fits neatly and safely into the space we have allocated to it. There it stays, just another of the 'coffee table books'—to dress up our living-room rather than address our lives. Perhaps we know in our heart of hearts that if we did accept the whole, including the parts we do not like or understand, it would mean a new way of life, and that would be dangerous!

Some of the Jewish authorities knew that what Jesus said was true. The light did break upon them, but they turned away because their own way of life without Jesus was more comfortable than with him. They did not want any trouble, so they kept quiet. They knew the truth all right, but that was as far as it went. What other people thought of them mattered more than God. 'They loved the approval of men rather than the approval of God.' What sad words. What a condemnation!

Something I find very fascinating when I visit a new place is reading old epitaphs in the churches and churchyards. They provide a valuable insight not only into the lives of particular individuals, but into the society of their time. Some read like character references, the life of the departed being described in such glowing terms. Like references, they often have to be read between the lines! The ones that really say something positive are not the glowing accounts of the achievements of the departed, but those with just a simple cross or a word of scripture, that bears a challenge to the living.

Perhaps none of us will have any say as to what is carved on our headstone; it will be left to those who have to see to such arrangements, unless of course we have left instructions in our will! Whether what is written is the opinion of our friends or the instructions we left behind doesn't really matter. What matters is the approval or disapproval of God. He will not write it on our tombstone. He will face us with it when we meet him.

Will you have the approval of God when you stand before him? Will I? I know this—as I look at my life, I do not have the confidence to hold it before God and say, 'Look what I have done; what I have achieved; what others have said about me!' But I take heart and confidence from what Jesus promised. I will be accepted by God because I have put my faith and trust in Jesus, 'who loved me and gave himself for me'. In the words of Charles Wesley:

> *No condemnation now I dread;*
> *Jesus, and all in him, is mine!*
> *Alive in him, my living Head,*
> *And clothed in righteousness divine,*
> *Bold I approach the eternal throne,*
> *And claim the crown, through Christ my own.*

The authority I have for this is Jesus! His promise to me. His promise offered and accepted.

Jesus offers life. He has been offering it for two thousand years. Always there are those who refuse his offer, who do not believe him, in spite of the evidence. Then there are those who believe him but consider other things of more importance—like status, a quiet life, money in the bank, an absorbing hobby, the demands of the family, the pressure of the job, the power of high office... But then, we have the choice. It all depends on what we really want—in the end.

# CHAPTER 8

# Be my guest

## JOHN 13:1–20

It has been the inspiration of artists, musicians and writers. It is seen as a symbol of love and unity, and also of division and rejection. The wise and learned seek to explain it, the humble accept it with awe and wonder. It is re-enacted wherever the name of Jesus Christ is known; and as you read this, men and women in many different places and circumstances will be taking part in the portrayal of what happened two thousand years ago in an upper room in Jerusalem.

Because, for Christians, what happened in that room was the embodiment of God's purpose for humankind, made known in Jesus Christ. They each look at the event and make it what they desire. Many have taken the mystery of that occasion and translated it, sought to confine it to the level of human understanding. To emphasize its importance, it has been clothed with the magnificence of earthly power, embellished with the jewels of earth, expanded with human eloquence. It has been given glowing descriptive titles, like neon signs lighting up a West End show, the 'rave reviews' shouting to command attention, inviting us in to the performance. But sometimes it is so grand, so exclusive, so expensive, that although we long to share in it we are not deemed fit to enter; we are disqualified by being what we are; we could not cope with the regulations which must be complied with if we would enter and be part of it. Those 'in the know', those who belong, guard the door. They only allow us to watch the comings and goings of the participants, to get a glimpse as the door is opened for them, but that is all.

What did happen at that special meal? We will not find the answer to our questions by looking at forms and ceremonies, even by looking at artists' impressions or listening to glorious choral offerings. We can only find out for ourselves by going back to the beginning, by going into that upstairs room, taking our place at the table, accepting the host's invitation to the supper.

Some time ago my husband Peter and I were guests at a very special celebration. A couple of hundred of us sat down to a most delightful meal, and as it was fairly informal there was no seating plan; we just sat where we wanted. There were enough places for all the invited guests and we found ourselves with people, some of whom we knew well, some slightly, and most not at all. What we had in common was that we had all been invited by the host. We were his guests; he, and what he was, was our meeting point. It was quite fascinating chatting with other guests over the meal, discovering quite a bit about each other. By the end of the evening we had opened up to each other in quite a deep way. If it had not been for our host, I don't suppose I would ever have talked to some of those people. We were poles apart, yet it was surprising, once we did open up, just how much we had in common.

A week or so later, I met with a group of colleagues at a conference where we were re-enacting the Last Supper. We had to decide which disciple we felt was most like ourselves and take his place. In fact, we discovered, the disciples really fell into three types—the conformists, the revolutionaries and the reconcilers. And so we divided ourselves into those three groupings and made our group contribution to that dramatic portrayal of the Last Supper. It was a most fascinating exercise. There were some real surprises as to where people saw themselves, and it also revealed tensions within our conferences. Sparks began to fly, hurts were expressed, sides were taken. But the marvellous thing was that when we joined in sharing the bread and wine, as we both received from and gave to each other, we discovered concern and love for one another, because we realized we were 'all guests at the table of the Lord'.

The friends of Jesus were in the upper room by invitation; they were there purely because of Jesus. Each one wanted to be with him, to share in that most intimate experience of friendship, eating together. They put up with the fellow guests because they had to! No doubt there were those who felt that the presence of some of the others spoilt their enjoyment—a pity they had been invited, it would have been much better without them! All of them wanted to be the Number One guest, to sit in the place of honour, and to be accorded the service they required.

Perhaps it sounds rather strong to say that of all of them, yet it must have been so, for not one of them was willing to perform the service of attending the needs of the others, that very basic need of a wash. They all sat there with the dirt of the streets on their feet, no doubt all tired, hot, unfit to sit down to a meal, but all unwilling to make the move to serve. All were so concerned with themselves, with their position, that they denied themselves as well as the others the relief they needed. As a modern expression would put it, 'they cut off their noses to spite their faces'.

One of them, Judas, was no doubt preoccupied, lost in his own thoughts. He knew that soon he would be up and away on the traitor's path, away from Jesus, away from the circle of friends. Soon he would be slapped on the back for his betrayal; he would hold the bag of silver coins, his reward for delivering the goods; and with a kiss he would mark for death the one who offered life. Why should he do it? Surely, after all the time with Jesus, he knew the reality of love, had learned from personal experience that Jesus alone had the answer for humankind? Could it have been that Judas was impatient with Jesus? Perhaps he thought to spur him on by his action, by putting him into the position of publicly and finally convincing his enemies of who he was. Did Judas really see himself as a double agent? We do not know the real reason behind his betrayal, whether it was greed for himself or the desire for the glory of the Lord. But Jesus knew, and whatever Judas was, he loved him.

Jesus loved all his friends. The fact that soon he would be betrayed, denied and deserted made no difference. He loved them, and all he saw as he looked at them was their need of someone to come along with a basin of cool water, who would wash the dirt and grime of the road from them, would ease their hot and tired feet, so that they could relax and enjoy their meal without distraction. Without words or fuss, Jesus got up, fetched a basin, water and a towel, and did what needed doing. He met their need. A very ordinary situation—hot and dirty feet needed washing, and Jesus did what was necessary.

I suppose most of us respond to the dramatic, but not so easily to the mundane, yet equally needed, acts of kindness and consideration. A big disaster, a multiple pile-up, a fire destroys blocks of houses, and help pours in. We see on TV the horror of scenes of famine and drought, and we reach for our cheque books. The blond, blue-eyed child smiles at us from the screen and we are quick to send a donation to enable that special medical attention to be paid for. But what about the old lady who lives alone up the road? She is a bit odd, and the house—it doesn't half smell; and she wouldn't thank you for calling. And so you—and I—we don't. That young mum we see pushing her pram to the shops—no one seems to bother with her. She looks as though she has been in a fight with someone—her eye was a real shiner the other week—we have heard the chap who lives with her knocks her about, and he is a bit rough with the kids. But then, what are the social services for? If we start interfering and asking questions, we might find ourselves drawn into a situation which has nothing do with us. No, leave it to those whose job it is to care. Anyway, she won't starve. No one does in this country, not like those abroad who haven't a health service or social security.

There is not much glamour or excitement in visiting smelly old ladies, nor in inviting a young mum and her runny-nosed baby into your home for tea. After all, you don't want to get involved with other people's lives, and babies make such a mess! But then, there wasn't much glamour or excitement in washing a dozen pairs of hot, sticky feet, was there? But Jesus did it. And he had this to say: 'I have set an example for you, so that you will do just what I have done for you.' Somehow that sounds rather like a command—and it seems to be directed at those who sit down at the Lord's table, who receive his loving offering, who have accepted his invitation to 'be my guest', and who enjoy his company. It could be that he is saying it to you, and to me, if we count ourselves to be guests at his table. Couldn't it?

# CHAPTER 9

# *Could it be... me?*

## JOHN 13:21–38

The words came as a bombshell. 'One of you is gong to betray me.'

The friends looked at one another, stunned by the awful implications of what Jesus had just said. Of course, all of them knew that Jesus was in constant danger from those who opposed him—those who were jealous and afraid of him, who saw him as a threat to either their political or religious life. At any moment there might be a knock on the door, the command to 'Open up!' and Jesus could be arrested and taken from them by sheer brute force by men from outside. But to say that the enemy was within—one of them! Surely that was unthinkable, impossible?

How could anybody who had responded to the call of Jesus to be one of his special group of friends do such a thing? They had had three years of living together as a family of friends; three years of observing, day in, day out, the life of their Master, his public ministry, his private life, his relationship with God his Father. Each one of them knew his love and care for them, individually, having learned it at first hand from him, discovering what it meant to be part of the Kingdom of God. How could any of them betray the one they followed, respected and loved? Who could it possibly be?

Peter looked across to John sitting next to Jesus. Perhaps Jesus would tell John if he asked, so Peter motioned to John to ask him. Jesus did not name the betrayer, but gave a clue: 'I will dip some bread in the sauce and give it to him; he is the man.' But none of them grasped what Jesus was talking about. It never occurred to them that it was Judas.

In two of the other Gospel accounts, those of Matthew (26:20) and Mark (14:19), the question is put rather differently. The friends ask Jesus, 'You don't mean me, do you?'

Yes, they were jittery and anxious. Perhaps some of them thought back to times when they had questioned Jesus, when maybe niggles of doubt had crept into their minds, or they had been tempted to give up and go back home. It had not been easy. They had had some rough times, some close shaves with those who opposed Jesus. They must have looked into each other's faces to see if there was any telltale sign of guilt. They looked, too, into their own hearts, and wondered. 'Could it be me?'

One man was sure it could not be him. Peter was so sure of himself, he would rather die than betray his Master, and he was quick to say so. It came as a nasty shock to be told he would deny Jesus —and not once, but three times. That hurt him. But he would prove his loyalty, he was sure of that.

So, there was one man confident that it was not he who would betray Jesus, ten other men wondering whether it possibly could be them. And the remaining man? Well, Judas knew who Jesus was talking about all right, but he kept his cool; not a flicker of guilt passed across his face. He did not betray himself—but would Jesus betray him? If he had, Judas would have been a dead man; the others would have seen to that. But Jesus did not name him; rather, he gave him a place of honour and affection. He appealed to him with love, not anger. Up to the very last moment, Jesus still pleaded with Judas, and in such a way that the others would not realize just what was passing between them. Finally Jesus let him go, himself providing the way out; and Judas went out. The words of scripture put it so starkly: 'It was night.'

Judas chose the darkness. He turned from the light. Why? Jesus had given the answer to that question quite early in his ministry, when a Jewish leader called Nicodemus had come secretly at night to talk to him. Jesus had talked about judgment, and said, 'This is how the judgment works: the light has come into the world, but people love the darkness rather than the light, because their deeds are evil' (John 3:19).

Judas chose the darkness. It was his choice, even after seeing the light. How was it possible? Yet it happened. He accepted the bread from the one who was 'the bread of life', and still went out into the night, to his own destruction.

What about us? Could we ever betray Jesus by our words and actions? Do we ever wilfully turn our backs on him? We are privileged to share in the 'breaking of bread'—called by various names by different groups of Christians, but the name doesn't really matter. We all come by invitation to the Lord's table to receive the tokens of his love for us. But it is so easy to take it for granted; to take it lightly; to take it when we are deliberately going against all that it represents. We may be dressed in our Sunday best, saying all the right words, looking the part—but what is really going on inside us? As we leave the place of communion, are we in effect doing as Judas did and going out into the night, into the darkness?

In the Book of Common Prayer of the Church of England the conditions of receiving Holy Communion are most clearly laid out: 'Ye that do truly and earnestly repent you of your sins, and are in love and charity with your neighbours, and intend to lead a new life, following the commandments of God, and walking from henceforth in his holy ways: draw near with faith...' When you look at these conditions, and look at yourself, dare you come?

Can any of us say we are fit to come? A friend of mine was discussing this very point with me recently. She said, 'There are times when I know I am in the wrong frame of mind, and yet what would other people think if I did not go up to communion? I know, as well, that when I am at outs with everything and everybody, then I need it more than ever.'

I could see what my friend meant, for this has been my own experience as well. Yet I take heart when I remember that Jesus offered the bread to Judas as well as the others. It was the offer of love. If Judas had been open to it, maybe he would not have gone out into the night. But it seems that his heart was hardened, his mind was made up. While we do recognize our frailty, while we are still open, then there is hope.

The self-confident Peter and the not-so-sure ten all let Jesus down later, for a variety of reasons. But not from hardness of heart. Their hearts were still with Jesus, and so they could know again the joy of being with him, belonging to him, being sent out to serve him—and so can we.

So take heart! 'Draw near with faith!' For the one who is 'the bread of life' will sustain us and strengthen us for our journey through life, wherever that journey takes us.

Yet there is another condition. In receiving the 'bread of life', we are then bound to one another as fellow travellers. For Jesus says, 'I give you a new commandment; love one another. As I have loved you, so you must love one another.'

Not easy, is it? Loving all the others. I don't suppose it was easy for the friends in the upper room. After all, they were a very mixed bunch. They even suspected one another of treachery; they were not absolutely certain of the next man, even though they had been together for three years. As I look around 'the Church', whether in my own congregation in Selby, or at any gatherings of fellow Christians, and see those who join with me at the Lord's table, I sometimes wonder about some of them. Can they be trusted? Do they really belong to the Lord? Do I have to love them? The first two questions are not mine to ask or reply to; but the answer to the third question, 'Do I have to love them?' is inescapable. Jesus commands me to love them.

I want to question his command. 'Lord, you don't know them. They are so irritating and infuriating. They insist on their own way all the time. They get on my nerves!' Jesus says, 'Love them as I have loved you.' I really would prefer not to! I was complaining bitterly one day to David Bond, my former colleague, about someone whom I was finding most difficult to get on with and I said, rather crossly, 'The trouble is, I don't even like him.' To which David replied with a smile, 'You don't have to like him, Margaret, but you have to love him!'

Why should I? Why should I, indeed—except for the fact that Jesus loves me, and commands me to love wholeheartedly, regardless of how I feel about various individuals? Why should I? So that it will be evident that I belong to him. That is the proof that is looked for in me.

Put like that, it's quite simple and straightforward—but then the most important things usually are, aren't they?

# CHAPTER 10

# One way only

## JOHN 14

Why is it that when the world crashes about our ears, when everything we had planned on falls apart and we are in absolute confusion and despair, there is always some bright spark who slaps us on the back and says, 'Don't get worried and upset!' Of course they are trying to be helpful, to calm us down and cheer us up, but somehow those words, and others in similar vein, only make matters worse. The bright-eyed, smiling friend is likely to get his smile and words stuffed down his throat—which may in itself prove a more therapeutic exercise for us than the words of the would-be helper!

The friends of Jesus had every reason to be worried and upset. Jesus had been telling them he was about to go away and leave them. It was pretty clear to them that the net was closing in, that those who were out to get him were in a very strong position. What was more, Jesus had just told them that one of their number would betray him, and that Peter would deny he even knew him. What a prospect! All their hopes were dashed, everything loomed so large and frightening, and the one person whom they depended upon was leaving. Jesus urged them to go on believing in God, and to believe in him. He told them he was going on ahead to prepare the way for them, and promised to return again. He assured them that they would realize this was true, and would be able to see the way ahead themselves.

Thomas jumped in with both feet. He challenged Jesus bluntly: 'Lord, we do not know where you are going; so how can we know the way to get there?' Good point! Can you imagine setting out on a journey which is not even on the map, and trying to get to the right spot? You wouldn't know where to start from, which path to follow. It is only when we know the destination that we can travel with any hope. We can then use our maps, ask people who have been there before, and take the right bearings. But a journey into the unknown—it sounds more like a huge gamble, with only a million-to-one chance of being remotely on the right road.

Life does seem, for most people, a huge gamble. It has too many possibilities. There are many attractive roads which so easily turn out to be dead ends, exciting and enticing highways which can land us in real trouble. There are endless conflicting views, with so many and varied claims by personalities and organizations to be *the* way, that it seems sheer luck whether we make any real progress in life. We end by changing direction over and over again, going round in ever decreasing circles until we flop down with exhaustion, having got nowhere—fast!

Jesus was unperturbed by Thomas' questioning. 'I am the way, the truth and the life,' he said, and continued, 'No one goes to the Father except by me... You will know my Father also, and from now on you do know him and you have seen him.'

This was just too much for another of the friends, Philip, to take. It he could actually see the Father, then that would be fine. All this talk was so confusing. What he wanted was to see the Father; that would solve all his problems. Jesus gently, yet firmly, reproached Philip for asking such a question. Surely after all this time, Philip must have realized who Jesus was? Could it be that Philip just had not grasped that Jesus and the Father are one? If only people would grasp that and believe it, then they could ask anything in the name of Jesus, and God would grant it, because Jesus and his Father are one and the same—God. Not only this, but the Spirit would come to be the Helper, and the Spirit would reveal the truth about God—God the Father, God the Son and God the Holy Spirit.

The friends were still muddled and confused, still questioning. If this was so, they wanted to know, why were they privileged to receive the truth, and not the rest of the world? Here they were, a few ordinary men; and out there was a world which contained learned people, powerful people, religious people. So why was the greatest truth of all given to a small group in an upstairs room rather than in a blaze of glory to the world? The answer was that the truth was revealed to those who would obey Jesus because they loved him. They would get all the help they would need; it would all be made clear, it would all drop into place, because the Holy Spirit would be their teacher, and the wisdom he would impart to them would be the wisdom of God.

'Do not be worried or upset...' I read those words many times, most often to people who are at their wits' end, in an extremity of grief and pain, following the death of a loved one. Those words of Jesus are the words I choose to speak to those who mourn, those who stand at a graveside, who look into the darkness of the earth, and see only despair. I expect there are some who hear the words who think me a fool to read them; who would, if they were not so polite, throw them back at me and challenge me to prove them. Yet I continue to read them, and believe them. I offer them, not as sentimental idealism, but as assurance and hope. I point to Jesus, who with arms open wide stands as the eternal signpost—the signpost to the Father, the way provided by the Father, and the giver of the Holy Spirit, who will help them along the way to the Father.

Father, Son and Holy Spirit—how many books have been written, lectures delivered, sermons preached, on the great theological truths of the Holy Trinity! How many Sunday school teachers have struggled to explain, with the aid of a shamrock leaf, what 'three in one and one in three' is all about! One local preacher confided to me some time ago, 'I dread being asked to preach on Trinity Sunday. It is beyond me.' Yes, it is beyond me to explain—let others more learned and well trained in theological exposition do that. The best explanation I have found is that contained in the *Family Worship* book, formerly published by CPAS, where, in place of the Creed, three questions are asked, and three answers given.

*Do you believe in God?* I believe in God the Father who made me and all the world.

*Do you believe in Jesus Christ?* I believe in Jesus Christ, the Son of God who came to this earth to be my Saviour. He died for my sins on the cross, rose again from the dead, ascended to the Father in heaven and will come again in his glory as Judge of all people.

*Do you believe in the Holy Spirit?* I believe in the Holy Spirit whom God gives to all who trust in Christ. He makes me more like Jesus, guides and strengthens me in my daily life, and helps me to serve God in the family of the Church.

Father, Son and Holy Spirit, available for you and for me—that is the glorious truth, the good news for the little people and the big people; the household names and those who make up the un-known and unsung; the wise and the foolish. And all we have to do to know Father, Son and Holy Spirit is to trust the one who is the way, the truth and the life, to love and to obey him—just that!

This is not something only to be worked out in the mind—although we do well to try, for we need to grapple with theological truth—but we must clothe it with the flesh of experience. What matters is that we live it out, in love and obedience. If we will do this, we are given a very special gift, the gift of peace. Jesus gave it as his parting gift to those who would count themselves among his friends. It is not a peace that will allow us to shut out the world, its troubles or its joys. It will not relieve us of the ups and downs which are common to all. It will not contain us in a germ-free bubble, for we have to live in the world; we are part and parcel of humanity, not on our own personal desert island. It is the peace of God, the *shalom*, the wholeness of being at one with God, know-ing that past, present and future are safe because he holds us and takes us through it all.

To that little band of frightened men Jesus gave the precious gift of his *shalom*, so that when they were worried and upset, they could release their fears and anxieties and be at peace. They would have loved to have remained in that upper room with the Lord and Master for ever—what peace that would have been! Yet Jesus moved on immediately: 'Come, let us go from this place.' They had to leave that place which would always hold such special memories, where they had been washed and fed, where they had shared in such sacred moments with Jesus, and go out into the world—a tough, harsh, brutal world. But they would carry with them the *shalom* of God. It would never be taken away from them. It would remain for ever.

Often, in a place of beauty and quietness, when I experience the presence of the Lord in a very special way, I long to remain there for ever, undisturbed by the ugliness and noise. Within the warmth of Christian fellowship, perhaps in a house group in our parish, or at a conference of like-minded people living in community based on Jesus, I would like to close the gate on ordinary life, everyday life. I must admit I have a selfish and cowardly nature which, when I am perhaps at my happiest, makes me say—at least to myself—'I'm all right, Jack, blow you!' Why should I leave my peace and go out into a society which well may go on perfectly all right without me? Why ask for trouble?

Perhaps that close band of friends in the upper room would not have expressed themselves like I have, but I am pretty sure they felt the same! Yet they had to go out—and go out with confidence, secure in the love and power of God, given by Jesus, and with that bonus package of peace. To go out knowing they could turn to the Father at any time for help in Jesus' name; in the assurance, even though they had not begun to grasp its implications, that they were going out to do even greater works than Jesus had already done.

Those who have taken the promises of Jesus and acted upon them have found them to be gloriously true. Jesus himself never moved outside Palestine, he had addressed crowds numbering only thousands, healed only a fraction of a vast multitude of diseases, dealt with only a limited variety of problems. The world he lived in here on earth was small and restricted; it had yet to explode in all directions. The friends of Jesus in the last two thousand years have shared his good news with millions, using every modern means, not least the printed word in thousands of languages. Think too of radio and television. One broadcast can reach more people than most preachers would address preaching twenty-four hours a day for a hundred years.

Men and women have gone to the four corners of the earth to bring Jesus to others, and many, through dedicated medical care, have brought healing and new life to countless people. Day by day the barriers are broken; new technology and skills make miracles an every-minute affair. Those who go out today in the name of Jesus are backed up by every modern means of communication. They have the tools, the 'know how' and the advantage of two thousand years of growing experience. Jesus is the same 'yesterday, today and for ever'—but he is not static. He is alive and active, moving in today's world with power; using the same basic material, though— men and women who know and love him and who go out and share him.

So for me, too, there comes the call to 'get up and go'. To be refreshed by Jesus in the quietness and beauty, to experience his cleansing and renewing in fellowship, is to be put back on my feet again and again, so that I may be pushed out into the world. Those words of Jesus, 'Come, let us go from this place', are spoken to me also—21st-century middle-aged woman that I am! There's work to be done; there's a world out there. His words come to you, too, if you count yourself a friend of his. There's work for you to do—so, on your feet! Like all the followers of Jesus, past, present and to come, we go out with his words ringing in our ears: 'If you ask me for anything in my name I will do it... It is my own peace that I give you... Do not be afraid.'

# CHAPTER 11

# *Multiply or die*

## JOHN 15:1—17

For three years Jesus had shared his life with a small group of men. Each was called into a unique relationship with him. They were disciples—learners, students, pupils, apprentices—specially select-ed for the biggest job in history, to carry the good news into every part of the world. They were the A-team, the Number One group. If they failed, what chance was there?

Jesus had spent those three years teaching, preaching and heal-ing. He had addressed himself to individuals and to the crowds, but with this small group he had shared the deepest truths, had spent time developing the teaching and giving them insight con-cerning the Kingdom of God. Three years—the time taken for a student today to obtain a degree, from entering university or col-lege to graduation day. Three years for Jesus' pupils to graduate and to begin to produce results.

The last term was running out fast, the final examinations loomed ahead. One had already dropped out; now there were only eleven. What were their chances? What of the Master? He had to hand on his life's work to the team. Would they prove worthy of the last three years? Had they got 'stickability'?

Jesus had very little time left for final instructions. He spelled out the position they were in, the options open. He chose as his illus-tration one of the commonest visual aids around—the vine. It was grown all over Palestine. Everywhere they looked there were vines growing, some producing well and giving a tremendous return; but many had gone wild, producing only leaves, taking over the ground, taking goodness out from the soil, but worthless, only fit for a bonfire.

The image of the vine would be well known to those men who listened so intently to Jesus. Israel had been described by the prophets of old as an empty vine, active, rampant, but unproduc-tive. Sadly this had proved so in her history. Yet the vine was still the symbol of Jewish imagery; the desire of God's people was to be as a fruitful vine. God had dealt severely with his people, and still they went on showing the signs of life, yet producing nothing.

So Jesus uses the picture of the vine and proclaims in God's name—'I AM'—that he is the true vine and his pupils the branches. There are two essential requirements. The first is to be united with him, to be part of him. That means sharing his life, being at one with him, obeying his commands, allowing his life to flow through them. If they think they can go it alone, doing their own thing, they will be as useless as a broken-off branch, for when the branch is broken the life is severed and the branch dries up, rots away or is burnt—destruction is its destiny.

It is not enough, though, merely to belong, to be a passenger. The whole point of the vine branch is the fruit it bears. To do so it has to be cared for, vigorously pruned back, protected and fed; the fruit-bearing branches are valuable indeed! Nothing pleases any gardener more than to see the fruit hanging from the branches. It makes him proud of his work; he can enjoy the admiration of others; the fruit has brought him the glory and is proof that his labour has been blessed by success. He has plenty to sing and cheer about. Harvest time is party time, the celebrations go on and on... And then it is time to prune, to build up, to look forward to another bumper harvest. And so the cycle continues.

Two thousand years ago the symbol of the vine would have meant much more than for most of us today in our industrialized society. Yet we can see exactly what it means. 'Business is business', whether measured by the milk yield, the fruit crop or the assembly line producing the latest in washing-machines or cars. The figures determine whether the one-man concern or the multinational corporation stays in business or gets the chop. What matters is not whether it is a happy set-up, the premises are good, the workers are content; but whether there are results. Or, in footballing terms, it is goals in the back of the net that count!

Of course we know this, it's a fact of life. But have we grasped the fact of our Christian life? The same rules apply—production or destruction. Jesus says so!

Where does that leave you and me? The first question we must ask is whether we are part of Jesus, united in his body. Is his life flowing through us? 'Do I really belong?' There is only one way we can be united with him, and that is by accepting him as our Master, Saviour and Lord. But what about the other bit—bearing fruit, producing results, showing a profit? It sounds all rather commercial, rather too business-like; but then shouldn't we be business-like in God's service?

I was asked to give a paper at a conference, entitled 'Hindrances to Mission'. I made a list of all the things I thought proved hindrances to the mission of the Church, and a lengthy list I finished up with, including lack of training, shortage of time, insufficient funding, preoccupation with personal ambition and plain apathy! Yet as I looked at my list I realized that these were but the symptoms; the basic problems were unbelief and disobedience. Within our churches there are many who are unbelievers. They are paper members, pew-sitters, meeting-attenders, supporters in various ways—but unbelievers for all that.

Once, by way of illustration in a sermon, I quoted how many Christians there are in the world, intending to encourage our congregation, and show them they were part of something big! One man came up to me as I stood at the door after the service. 'You know that figure you quoted this morning, are they all really Christians or just church members?' I confessed the figure was probably derived from membership returns. 'But who would you say was a Christian, then?' he persisted, and then added, 'Would you say I was one?' I looked at him and said, 'You should know whether you are or not.' He did not reply, but since that conversation he has opened up much more. He is, I believe, on the road to faith, because he had to question where he himself stood with Jesus.

Yes, unbelief is sadly all too common in our churches, and perhaps those of us who stand in the pulpit week by week must bear the blame. We have assumed too much from counting attendances, or figures on the roll, rather than challenging those who are within our membership with the black-and-white facts of the gospel. We have allowed people to believe that they can enter the Kingdom of Heaven through good will, by having their names on a membership list, participating in church events, or clocking in to worship Sunday by Sunday.

And what of those who are Christians, who have a personal faith? Are they bearing fruit, or producing a good show of greenery?

Are you producing any fruit? What have you got to show for yourself?

Jesus spoke very directly to his group of pupils. If they did not go on to bear fruit, his work would have been in vain. They had to multiply or die. Thank God, they went on to bear fruit. The Church grew in leaps and bounds; the frontiers were pushed out; the good news was shared. They were obedient, they did as they were told. They willingly underwent the discipline and hardships, so that Jesus was honoured and accepted. Then others took up the challenge, and so they carried on through the centuries, bearing fruit. The price was high, but they paid it gladly.

The price is still high. Jesus demands our obedience, total obedience. Then we, too, will bear fruit. It will cost us everything, but in exchange what do we get? To be part of Jesus—his body. To share in his glory and his joy. And we graduate from being servants to being friends—and that makes all the difference in the world.

Part of my work when I was appointed Broadcasting Officer for the York Diocese included serving the Archbishop of York, who, for the first eight years of my appointment, was Dr Stuart Blanch. I did many radio interviews with him, and attended a multitude of press conferences and other events. I was also made Deaconess by him in York Minster, and promised to obey him 'in all things lawful and honest'. It was a great pleasure to serve him; whatever he asked me to do, I did gladly, not just because he was the Archbishop, but out of great personal affection for him. He was 'the boss', but more than that, he was my friend, and I could turn to him at any time. He was concerned for me as me, and not just as a broadcasting officer or a deaconess. To serve him was a privilege, to know his friendship was and is a joy.

Jesus offers us that same relationship with him: not just the privilege of service, but the joy of being his friend. Surely that is worth everything, bearing in mind the awful alternative?

# CHAPTER 12

# *You have been warned*

## JOHN 15:18—16:15

The world is wary of those who suggest that there is an alternative way of ordering society. New ideas can pose a threat to the established leadership, and people who claim to have discovered a way of life that will radically alter both the social structures and individuals are to be viewed with suspicion. Such people can prove dangerous, for they do not conform to accepted ways; and so it is thought better that they are removed from the scene, so that life can go on as normal, as dictated by the powers that be, and the way it has always been.

Jesus was such a person. He challenged every stratum of society —individually, politically, socially and in the most tender area of all, the religious life of his day. He trod on the toes of the Establishment, until gradually embarrassment turned to disapproval, then to hatred. Time and time again, attempts were made to get rid of him, to destroy him and his message. This also applied to those who followed him; they too were dangerous and posed a threat, so they must be eliminated.

Jesus tells his friends plainly what the situation is: 'If the world hates you, remember that it hated me first.' He goes further, with an even more painful announcement: 'You will be expelled from the synagogues, and the time will come when anyone who kills you will think that by doing this he is serving God.' Not a pleasant prospect, to be hated by the world, by those who had no time for religion— but also by those who should have been a support, their fellow Jews. What chance their survival against such overwhelming odds?

The friends of Jesus would soon experience what he had warned them about. They would undergo persecution from many quarters, not least from those who were God-fearing, religious people, and from their leaders. Perhaps that would be the hardest to bear, to be hated by those who should have realized who Jesus was and received him with joy.

It has never changed. The words of Jesus ring down through the centuries: 'They will do all this to you because you are mine.' Anne Arnott, in her account of the life of John Bunyan, *He Shall With Giants Fight* (Kingsway, 1985), describes the dreadful persecution Bunyan endured, and from those who thought they were doing God's will in their treatment of that holy man who gave us *Pilgrim's Progress*. She reminds us that he was 'ever to be remembered for his heroic stand as a prisoner of conscience whose one desire was to witness for his Lord'.

There have been, and still are, many prisoners of conscience witnessing for their Lord in spite of hatred and persecution. Many have risked and even given their lives—good, saintly men and women, whose only crime has been to serve Jesus Christ. People like Archbishop Janani Luwum of Uganda, murdered, as were so many Ugandan Christians during the Amin regime. Like many Christian leaders in South Africa, such as Archbishop Desmond Tutu, who suffered continual harassment. Like Bishop Dehqani Tafti of Iran, whose son was murdered, and who narrowly escaped with his own life. And what of the thousands of nameless Christians in places like southern Sudan, Pakistan and Indonesia, suffering today because of their faith?

Come nearer to home, to the situation in Northern Ireland, where Christians, both Catholics and Protestants, who work for peace and understanding based on the love of Jesus are misunderstood, rejected and often in danger from those they try to help. In mainland Britain, many ministers and their families, particularly in the cities, are victims of violence. A friend of mine, a vicar in Hull, arrived late for a meeting. He apologized and explained, 'Sorry I'm late, but we were burgled yet again last night, and the vicarage was vandalized.' Church buildings are often the subject of vandalism, their furnishings destroyed, defaced or stolen. Those who speak out in the media, especially on moral issues, are constantly subjected to abusive telephone calls and letters. These are just some examples of what happens when people are prepared to stand up and be counted as followers of Jesus.

In the Church of England baptism service, the child—or it may also be an adult—is signed with the sign of the cross and then charged with these words: 'Do not be ashamed to confess the faith of Christ crucified. Fight valiantly under the banner of Christ, against sin, the world, and the devil, and continue his faithful soldier and servant to the end of your life.' It's a reminder that following Jesus is no easy option, for Christians swim against the tide; and sin, the world and the devil will try to pull them back and under.

So with so much pressure, what chance have we got? How can we cope? The fact of the matter is that we cannot cope. We cannot win the battle on our own, not even the strongest of us. But help is at hand, from the Holy Spirit, the one who is 'the Helper'.

For the friends of Jesus, the promise of the Holy Spirit would not take away the fear, the sadness and the confusion of that moment. So much was happening to them, everything was in turmoil; all they knew was that Jesus was leaving them. They would be alone in an alien world and, if anything, things would get worse. As yet, the Holy Spirit was beyond their experience or understanding. There was a limit to what they could take in at that time. Jesus wanted to tell them so much more, but he knew they could not take it: 'I have much more to tell you, but now it would be too much for you to bear.' So he just reminds them again that help will come. Then they will understand; they will be given power to rise above fear and hatred, above death itself.

In time, those friends would begin to understand what Jesus had been telling them all the time he was with them. Gradually they would become aware of the meaning of things that had happened during their three years 'on the road' with him. Things that puzzled them would suddenly become gloriously clear, and the memories of the past would become entrances into a totally new understanding of the Kingdom of God. But all this was in the future; they had to live through the present.

There are times when life does not make sense, when we cannot understand what is happening to us. Part of us cries out for the answers, wanting to know what will happen tomorrow, next week, next year. There are those who turn to fortune-tellers—to those they hope will unravel the future for them. How sad, and how dangerous this is! What good would it do to know, even if it were possible to know? When, early in his ministry, Jesus talked to the people on the hillside about being anxious about what was to come, he said, 'So do not worry about tomorrow; it will have enough worries of its own' (Matthew 6:34). In other words, live a day at a time. And as my vicar is always telling me, when I push towards what I think ought to be done this very minute and which actually is perhaps days or even weeks ahead: 'That's tomorrow's problem!' Help will come. It will be given when we need it, and when the time is right we will begin to understand. Then everything will fall into place, for the Helper who Jesus promised his friends would come, has come, and he will lead you and me into all the truth we need, at the right time.

I find it hard to wait. I want to know everything *now*! That is part of my very impatient nature. And yet how gently Jesus deals with me, and reminds me that it is in his time and not mine that I will understand. Not because he wants to withhold things from me, but because he knows me, and knows my limits. Archbishop William Temple puts it so sensitively in his *Readings in St John's Gospel* (Macmillan, 1940) when he says, 'The disciple is not to clamour for the solution of perplexities or for intellectual mastery of divine mysteries. What knowledge he has in this realm is his because the Spirit has declared it to him; and for the Spirit's declaration he must wait.'

Wise words to the impatient, puzzled, 'let's get up and go' disciple, who says, 'I want to know, and I want to know *now*.' Maybe I am beginning to learn to wait, although rather impatiently. The fact that I know 'the Lord is here; his Spirit is with us' assures me that everything will be all right, in spite of the way it may seem at this moment.

Waiting is hard—but the answers are worth waiting for!

# CHAPTER 13

# '...But it was worth it!'

## JOHN 16:16-33

I came to motherhood rather late—in fact I was thirty, and in the eyes of the medical profession 'at risk' because of my age and various complications I acquired during pregnancy. The baby was overdue and so steps were taken to induce the birth. It was mid-January in one of the coldest, snowiest years on record, the hospital was one of the oldest in the country, and the pipes froze, the heating went off, and at one stage the lighting failed. Going into labour in that situation was anything but pleasant, and it was long and protracted. Finally, in the middle of the night, our son was born, a forceps delivery. It had been difficult, dangerous and painful, but nothing could equal the sound of that baby crying as he came into the world, and the congratulatory words of the doctor, 'You have a son.' The thrill of a bundle being placed in my arms, the bundle that was Julian Peter Cundiff. Later, wheeled back into the ward of sleeping women, I was so excited that I woke the woman in the next bed and proudly announced, 'I've had a baby.' 'Have you, luv, I am pleased,' was her reply! By early morning when the tea came round I had written a pile of letters, filled in all the cards which were to go to relatives and friends, and I felt I had the energy left to climb Everest!

Three years later our daughter Alison arrived. She had the sense to arrive in May, in a newly opened, ultra-modern hospital, and at tea time! But the thrill was just the same, following an anxious time, though thankfully not quite as bad as with our son. Any mother will recognize in what I have described her own experience of 'before' and 'after'—the anxiety, the pain, the struggle, yet all forgotten in the joy of birth. Every mother feels at the moment of delivery that she is the only person in the world to have accomplished so much. Even winning a gold medal in the Olympics could not be more exhilarating.

Jesus used that illustration of childbirth to explain to his friends what they would have to go through in the next few days. He knew that ahead of them lay great sadness, suffering and fear. The pain for him would be so much more; but he had the assurance of his Father, whom he knew and trusted. Even though he shrank from what was to come, he accepted it because he knew it was the way to life and glory. If he could have, he would have gone through the suffering of his friends too. But, like childbirth, each one must go through it for themselves; there is no other way. When a new life comes into the world it comes through pain to birth, to joy. The Jewish people used the picture of childbirth to describe the coming of the new age, when the Messiah would appear. They knew he would burst through the agony barrier, gloriously bringing in his kingdom. Yet they did not realize that the time of delivery had arrived, it was upon them; and so they lost out on the triumph of God.

Sadness and joy are interwoven. The pain of parting, for those who love each other, is so intense; but what joy is there to compare with that of reunion? One of the young men from our church, a sailor, served in the Falklands. I well remember the sadness and anxiety we all felt as he went from us; the agonizing time, particularly for his family and his fiancée, when it was announced that his ship had been sunk, and it was not yet known who had survived. Nothing could describe those hours of waiting, the blackness and despair we all felt. But then came the telephone call that confirmed he had been picked up. He was alive! There were plenty more tears shed, but this time they were tears of joy, and there were even more as he came home to one of the best parties ever. For me the delight was to be even greater a year later, when I assisted at the wedding of Terry and Judith, and in the vestry I was gathered into the arms of the handsome young sailor in uniform, proudly wearing his Falklands medal. The first woman he kissed as a married man was the deaconess—closely followed by the bride! Yes, life is made up of sorrow and joy, anxiety and relief, agony and ecstasy.

Jesus used many homely illustrations to explain great spiritual truths. Every preacher and teacher does the same. Examples drawn from what we know and understand lead us to see beyond, and will shed new light on something that confuses us. Then the time comes when we need no illustration, for the light has dawned; we understand the truth. Jesus had often spoken in parables, so that the light would filter in through the darkness. Soon there would be no more need for illustrations. The great visual aids of all time would be seen—that of the cross, for it would speak for ever of the unlimited love of God, and the empty tomb which would speak of the power and victory of love. The Holy Spirit would come in love and power and fill men and women with the spiritual force that they would need for the new age.

But this was still in the future. Those friends of Jesus had yet to discover the power of the Holy Spirit, but for now their questions were answered, even the unspoken ones. Jesus had looked into their hearts and answered them. They now knew that everything Jesus had told them was true. They were convinced.

They were convinced now—but Jesus knew that soon they would doubt, they would run away, they would fail; but only for a time. Gently he warned them what would happen. He knew they would run away and fail, but when it happened he wanted them to remember that he would know, he would understand, he would still love them and they could be at peace, knowing that everything was under control. Suffering lay ahead, but Jesus had already won the victory. The world would do its worst, but nothing could separate them from him, and from his Father, who was their Father.

Later on, a man named Saul, a man very much of the world, feared by those who followed Jesus because of his persecution campaign against Christians, would become a follower of Jesus. He would himself experience hatred, persecution and great suffering, yet he would become the greatest influence ever for Jesus. Saul the persecutor became Paul the great missionary and apostle. He eventually took the good news of Jesus even to Rome. His letters have been the means of countless men and women coming to know Jesus, even to our own century. Men and women have been inspired to go on following Jesus in spite of the pain, the persecution, the scorn of the world. Paul could triumphantly say, 'Who, then, can separate us from the love of Christ? Can trouble do it, or hardship or persecution or hunger or poverty or danger or death? ... No, in all these things we have complete victory through him who loved us!' (Romans 8:35–37).

Paul put into words what millions have discovered to be true, that Jesus has won the victory. Many have gone to their death with the words of Jesus ringing in their ears: 'The world will make you suffer. But be brave! I have defeated the world!'

For most of us, the suffering we have to go through will be nothing compared with those who have given their lives, who have died heroically as martyrs. Yet we are all called to suffer. We all experience our little deaths in the world. We all plumb the depths at times—maybe through fear, depression, doubt, ridicule, snide remarks, the cold shoulder, rejection by those who we hoped would have understood. The words of Jesus come to renew our courage and our hope. They rally us to our feet, they beckon us home: 'I have defeated the world!'

Secure in that knowledge, what have we to fear?

# CHAPTER 14

# Listen—he's praying for you

## JOHN 17

Now it was time to move, out from the intimate meeting place, away from that room which had enclosed them in love and fellowship, where they had experienced for the last time the joy of being together, sharing a meal. That meal would be re-enacted until the end of time, with its sharing of heart and mind and spirit. Jesus had shared with his friends in the deepest possible way. He had sought to prepare and equip them for what lay ahead. Soon he would be leaving them; the future would lie with that small group of bewildered and anxious men.

As they rose to their feet to go out into the world's arena, to 'go public', Jesus stopped, lifted his eyes to heaven and began to pray. I can feel the atmosphere, I can see those friends of Jesus with their eyes on him, silently watching and waiting as they realize that they are witnessing not just a man at prayer, but a Father and Son bound together in love—God the Father and God the Son.

To read the seventeenth chapter of John's Gospel is to stand listening with those friends of Jesus in silence, in wonder. It is also to be enfolded in the security of love. It is a glimpse of glory that is now and is to be, a glory that we share in.

'Jesus looked up to heaven...' Perhaps those who stood and watched him remembered him standing outside the tomb of his friend Lazarus, when he prayed then that the glory of God might be seen as the dead man was brought back to life. They would remember how immediately that glory was seen as Lazarus emerged from the grave, alive, strong, free. God's glory was powerfully seen as death was conquered, flung aside in defeat, like the rejected grave clothes.

'Jesus looked up to heaven...' The cross lay ahead, but so did the glorious victory. The thanksgiving had already begun as Father and Son met together. Jesus had shown the glory of God from the beginning of his life on earth, and he would leave the world in the blaze of God's glory. He could say, 'I have finished the work you gave me to do.' No wonder he had such a sense of completeness with his Father.

Perhaps we all know in a small way, at times, that sense of completeness when we successfully finish a job. It may be a very simple thing, or an exhausting programme which has drained us of our energy, taken all our time, strained us to the limits. Writing a book is a bit like that—it is for me, at any rate. The demands of a time schedule, the burning of the midnight oil, struggling to be able to put the right words on to the paper, coping with the irritation of interruptions when I am in the middle of something that is beginning to flow, and taking with a smile the remarks of well-meaning friends who do not see the point of the book anyway. Yet all is forgotten as the manuscript is handed over, the deadline met. Later, when the manuscript is actually a book on the shelves, bought and read, it is all worthwhile. There is a sense of achievement, the satisfaction of finishing the job, producing the work and seeing the smile on the face of my editor!

I do not think it is irreverent to compare simple human endeavour with how Jesus must have felt as he met his deadline and knew his Father's pleasure. How did God the Father feel? Do you ever wonder that? I can only speak again as a parent, remembering my children as youngsters. I recall the joy and the pleasure I felt as I saw my son, dark rings under his eyes from the long hours of study, because he had been poring over his books rather than out in the open air enjoying his fishing, waving his final essay in the air and saying, 'Mum, it's finished!' Or my daughter proudly carrying in the cake she had made and iced for Christmas, announcing, 'Look, it's finished. Do you like it?'

A book, an essay, a cake—all these very ordinary human things give me a taste of glory, and point me to the one of whom John could write '...and we beheld his glory'.

Jesus and his Father were in complete harmony; and because of their relationship we can know God, and so know eternal life. The word 'know' here has a much deeper meaning than simply acceptance of a truth, such as a knowing that two and two make four, or C-A-T spells cat. William Temple says, in *Readings in St John's Gospel*:

*The word for 'know' here is not that which stands for a grasp of
truth; it is that which stands for personal acquaintance. Even in
human relationships there is the constant delight of new discover-
ies by each in the character of the other. Eternity cannot be too long
for our finite spirits to advance in knowledge of the infinite God.*

In this prayer we see the Father and Son relationship; and we also
see Jesus the representative, the 'great high priest'. He enters into
his Father's presence on others' behalf too! As his friends listened
to his prayer, they would suddenly become aware that Jesus was
bringing them into his Father's presence, into that holy of holies.
He presented them to his Father with joy and thanksgiving. He
asked his Father to keep them safe. He asked his Father to protect
them—not to take them out of the world, but to keep them safe
within it, so that they too might show his glory. Jesus had given
his friends everything; now he entrusted them to his Father. His
friends could never forget that prayer; it would be written on their
hearts. And as Jesus prayed, it would bring them joy and peace and
hope, even in the dark days ahead, even to the end of their lives.

What a unique privilege to be brought to God in prayer by Jesus!
What assurance it must have given those friends that they, ordinary men, had been considered important enough, had been loved
enough, for Jesus to be concerned to the extent that he shared his
concern for them with his Father. As the friends listened, they must
have been filled with love for Jesus as they heard him pray for
them. It must have enthused them with the determination to live
out his prayer, to be the people he wanted them to be.

And Jesus didn't finish there. He went on, 'I pray not only for
them, but also for those who believe in me because of their
message.' Do you realize who Jesus was praying for then? Has it
dawned on you who he meant? Do you believe in Jesus? Have you
come to know him, maybe through the witness of a friend, or
within a Christian family? After hearing a preacher, reading a book,
seeing a film or being faced with words of scripture on a poster? We
come to know Jesus through the witness of others, through the
faithfulness of generations. We are able to read the word of God because of the faithful witnesses who wrote it. We read it in our own
language because of the faithfulness of translators, printers and
distributors. We can hear God's word because of the faithfulness of

those who have preached and proclaimed that word, who have shared the good news. We will never know, this side of heaven, how many links have been in the chain of our coming to know Jesus. For them and for us, for you and for me, Jesus prayed.

How do you feel, knowing that? It makes me want to do all I can to help answer his prayer. He prayed that you and I might be one, of the same mind and heart as him and as each other. I often hear people speak disparagingly about 'ecumaniacs'—they pour cold water on schemes for Christian unity and refuse to be involved in united acts of witness and sharing. Yet Jesus prayed that we might all be one. Not a uniformity that is so bland and colourless that it has no taste or use, but the oneness which Jesus and his Father enjoyed. We are to be one—'all one in Christ Jesus'. And that includes being one with our Christian brothers and sisters of other cultures, colours, languages. We are to be so much at one with them that we would give our very lives for them.

We are called to be at one with those who are closest to us within the organizations of the church, the home groups, the fellowship meetings; with those who serve alongside us on the church council, the elders' meeting or on one of that multitude of committees that are both the bane and blessing of church life. Perhaps here lies the greatest obstacle to our oneness. It is so difficult to be at one with those we rub shoulders with day in, day out—the rubbing along together can cause some very nasty friction burns! There is a tension born of being closely involved with each other in the church; it is because we are each so sure we have all the answers, and are the answers! The problems arise as other people think exactly the same about themselves! We are all guilty; we are given more to individuality than to oneness with the others.

The friends of Jesus were just the same as us. They had to live and work together. They were a varied bunch of individuals; oneness did not come easily to them. There were petty quarrels, misunderstandings, hidden resentments. There were flare-ups, party spirit, the desire for one-upmanship. Human nature does not change! And the Church is full of human nature in the raw!

Sadly, how we behave towards each other is seen not only by those within the Church, but by those outside. Our witness is not to being all one, but to being fragmented and divided. Sometimes the verdict of the world is not, 'See how these Christians love one another,' but, 'See how they hate one another.' Because of the intensity of our feelings, which we believe are one hundred per cent right, we easily hurt each other. And those hurts can fester and destroy, unless we allow them to be dealt with by the one who prayed so passionately for us that we might be one. To be all one in Jesus is no easy matter; it will cost us dearly. But however high the price, it will never approach the price Jesus paid for us to be at one with him and his Father.

At a service in York Minster in 1986, Catholics, led by Cardinal Basil Hume, joined with Anglicans in commemorating the 400th anniversary of the martyrdom of Margaret Clitherow, a York butcher's wife killed by other Christians for refusing to renounce her Catholic faith. The then Archbishop of York, Dr John Habgood, said in his sermon:

> *Our religious impulses have to be brought again and again to the place of forgiveness. The things that can so easily distort religious commitment—pride and fear and self-seeking and humbug—have to be offered up and given back to us by God as faith and hope and love. The lust for certainty, the need to be right, the wish to dominate and control, have to be brought to the cross of Christ and endure the searching gaze of one who died helpless and forsaken. The religious fortress mentality which keeps us separated from one another and ultimately tempts us to make martyrs of one another has to be broken down.*

Jesus' prayer was that we might know the joy of being one with him and with each other, and witness by our lives the reality of that oneness. Will we ever all be one? I believe the answer lies not in great schemes, although it is right that we should continually strive for unity with all the Christian traditions, but in learning to love unreservedly our fellow Christians in the local situation. When people in the world around see the Jesus-quality of love in your life and mine, then there's a chance they may listen to what we have got to say.

When Jesus had finished praying, he and his friends walked down the valley, across the brook Kidron, and into a place where they had spent many happy times together. It was a garden; a place of peace and quiet, a place in which to enjoy the company of friends. It would be anything but peaceful and quiet this time. It was here that the paths of Jesus and his friends would part company; and the garden would go into the record books as the place where Jesus was betrayed by a friend. The name of the garden was Gethsemane.

# CHAPTER 15

# What sort of man could do that?

## JOHN 18:1–11

The account of the arrest of Jesus in the garden of Gethsemane contains elements that puzzle me. There are features which are hard to understand. It is like trying to fit one of those wooden puzzle balls together without having the small central piece. Those relevant features were probably so obvious to those who were there at the time that it was not felt necessary to record them. After all, everybody knew the situation at the time; and would they have thought that two thousand years later people would have been reading of the arrest of Jesus and puzzling over a very simple point?

Yet each time I read of the arrest, these questions arise in my mind. Why did the authorities have to go to all the trouble of paying an informer to betray Jesus? After all, Jesus was well known. He did not go around in disguise; he did not hide away. He was not surrounded by a private army.

Why did they send so many armed men, both Roman soldiers and temple guards, to pick up one unarmed man? It seems to me a very involved way of dealing with a simple matter. But then I wasn't there! What is clear is that it happened the way the New Testament said it did. All four Gospel accounts record it—obviously seen through different eyes so that there are some minor points which differ—but all record the place, the manner of arrest and the events which followed.

Jesus was with his friends in the garden, a place they often visited to enjoy, to wander in, to talk together in a pleasant spot, just as most of us enjoy walking in our own or other people's gardens, strolling around, relaxing in natural beauty. Then suddenly the place was full of armed men, with lanterns and torches. It could have been that they were armed because they were afraid of Jesus;

after all, they would know he had the power to work miracles—there was plenty of evidence of those. Could it be that he was possessed of great personal strength, more than any other man? Did he carry a secret weapon? Had he even a secret army that would spring out of the darkness to protect him? These were all possibilities that must be catered for. On the other hand, hearing their approach, he might flee from them and hide. He knew the area well, and there had been times before when he had seemed almost to melt away from sight. So lanterns and torches would be needed to aid their search. One thing was sure, they meant to find him and overpower him; so that is why they went out with so many men, why they carried with them weapons, torches and lanterns. They were ready for anything, they had all possibilities covered—it was a military operation.

Jesus could, of course, try to pass himself off as someone else—those loose eastern garments would aid his disguise; in the rush he would look like any other Jewish male, aged around thirty. Ah, but they had thought about that one as well! Judas, one of his closest friends, had agreed to point him out to them, to approach him. Then it would be a simple matter quickly to overpower him, tie him up and take him away.

What actually happened was all very different from what they had expected. So different, it threw them completely. Jesus asked them who they were looking for, and when they replied, 'Jesus of Nazareth', he calmly announced, 'I am he.'

Their response was strange in the extreme, for they moved back and fell on the ground. Think about that! All those armed men falling back and over, and Jesus just standing there unarmed, unhidden. What was it in his manner that made them afraid? Could it have been that they suddenly realized that here was no ordinary man? Here was someone who could wipe the lot of them off the face of the earth if he wanted to. Here was the one who spoke like God, using the name of God, 'I AM'. In a modern expression, he put 'the fear of God' in them!

Jesus just stood there. His only request was that the friends he had with him be allowed to leave. After all, they were not needed. But Peter was all for making a fight of it and hit out wildly, cutting off the ear of the high priest's servant. He was at once rebuked by Jesus, and in the account of Luke, the doctor, we read that Jesus reached out and touched the man's head and healed him.

Jesus was perfectly in control of events. He was the one who was calm, and at peace. This alone must have unnerved the others in the garden, including Judas. Or could it have been that Judas was sure Jesus would have called the angels to his aid, shown his power, demonstrated dramatically who he was? Perhaps he was waiting to see it happen before aligning himself again as one of the friends. Jesus did demonstrate who he was, but not in the way expected; and Judas, the traitor, must have realized to his horror that he had betrayed the person who was the best friend he ever had. He had thrown away everything for thirty pieces of silver. It had all gone horribly wrong. It is recorded in one of the other Gospel accounts (Matthew 27:3–9) that Judas took back the money to the chief priests and said, 'I have sinned by betraying an innocent man to death!' but there was no comfort for Judas. No one cared; he was rejected; no one wanted to know him. And so, absolutely distraught and convicted of his sin, he went and did what, sadly, many people in their extremity do—he killed himself.

If only he had realized before he had changed sides what he was doing! If only he had grasped what Jesus had been telling him right up to the last moment! If only... if only...

There is a story told which is thinking ahead to the end of time. The storyteller describes Jesus sitting with eleven of his friends at table. The meal is ready, but they seem to be waiting for someone to join them. Then there is a knock at the door, and Judas comes in and stands before Jesus with downcast eyes. 'Come in, my friend,' says Jesus. 'We were waiting for you.'

Yes, I know that story is an imaginary one—and yet, knowing Jesus, knowing his love, could it not be true?

There is a streak of Judas in us all. We want things our way, and when they don't go our way we try to manipulate things and people. We push them to the limit; and sometimes, tragically, as for Judas, everything goes wrong. We, too, crash headlong, and there seems no hope, no help, no way back. I remember, years ago, singing an old gospel song. It has always stuck in my mind, for it is the message of hope even in seeming hopelessness:

*There's a way back to God from the dark paths of sin;*
*There's a door that is open and you may go in:*
*At Calvary's cross is where you begin,*
*When you come as a sinner to Jesus.*

**E.H. Swinstead (Copyright control)**

There is a way back for all of us, and the 'if onlys' can be wiped away if we are willing to come in penitence for the past, coming to Jesus and allowing him to lift us up and bring us back into the circle of his friends.

Judas is a figure to take heed of. He reminds us that even one who had been so close to Jesus could turn away, could be an instrument of destruction. 'What sort of a man could do that?' we ask ourselves in horror. The answer is, someone like you and me. We need to recognize our own weakness, wilfulness and blindness. But at the same time we must take courage; there is a way back, as long as we are willing to take it. The door is open; we have to go through, and accept the love and the forgiveness that await us. Sadly, Judas went to the wrong place with his confession and remorse. If only he had gone to Jesus, things would have been so different for him.

Yes, you and I have a lot to learn from the life of Judas—and when the danger signals flash in our lives, let's make sure we stop and listen.

# CHAPTER 16

# What would you have done?

## JOHN 18:12–27

We all jump to conclusions—very quickly—and often hold on to those snap conclusions permanently. We sum people up in a moment and we are bound to our decisions, without ever asking whether we really did have all the facts. Many a person has been damaged for life by an opinion publicly passed by someone who jumped in without knowing anything of the background. Some of the more popular daily newspapers have much to answer for in the way they sloganize people in the news. The headlines over-emphasize the seemingly obvious, and once someone has been headline news it is difficult ever to escape from that picture implanted in the minds of those who read the headlines and, without thinking, accepted them as true.

What about Peter? How do you think of him? Peter the impetuous, Peter the coward, Peter the boss. I tried a small experiment some time ago, and asked a number of people at random what they knew about Peter. Without exception they mentioned first of all, 'He denied Jesus three times'—that is, of course, those who knew anything at all about him!

So maybe we could all do with taking another look at Peter before we also brand him as a coward and a person of no 'stickability'.

We are told that Peter and another disciple followed Jesus when he was arrested; they wanted to see where Jesus was being taken, and what was going to happen. Rather than running away, they kept close, as close as they could. What would you have done? I fear I would have run as fast as my legs would have carried me away from the trouble, thankful to escape, wanting only the safety of home and the opportunity to think about my next move. Not Peter and his companion—they were prepared to stick close by Jesus. Could it be that they hoped to 'spring' him or find out if there was any chance of a rescue mission?

The friend who was with Peter is unnamed. Tradition has it, and it would seem very well attested, that it was John, not naming himself out of a genuine humility and not wanting to boast that he stuck by Jesus when others had fled. It seems that John was able to gain admittance to the high priest's house because he was known. Perhaps he had delivered fish there in the past—his father's business was salt fish—and so the family would be no strangers to the household of the high priest. Whether that can be proved one hundred per cent I am not sure, but it is a likely explanation for his being known and allowed in, and being able to bring Peter in also.

They put themselves in a very dangerous position indeed, for they were in enemy territory. The servant girl who let them in looked at Peter and seemed to remember she had seen him before—hadn't she seen him around with Jesus? So she asked him, probably not in an accusing way, but merely curious. 'Aren't you also one of the disciples of that man?'

For the first time Peter was challenged about his relationship with Jesus. 'No, I am not!' he said. He denied that he belonged to the company of the friends of Jesus.

Before you judge him harshly, think again—what would you have done? Changed your mind about going in, perhaps? Peter walked even closer to danger. He stood by the fire with the servants of the high priest, with the soldiers on guard duty. The firelight would show him up even more clearly, and yet he stood there. But soon he was challenged again, this time by a number of them. Again Peter was adamant and again denied he was one of the disciples.

But then someone who had been in the garden of Gethsemane, a relative of the man whom Peter had struck with his sword, looked at him closely and asked, 'Didn't I see you with him in the garden?' Here was real trouble, for Peter could have been arrested for attacking another person, regardless of whose company he kept.

'No,' insisted Peter; by now he must have been petrified. And at that precise moment a cock crowed. Whether it was an actual cock crowing or the 3.00 a.m. trumpet call which was known as 'cock-crow' doesn't really matter. Peter knew then that what Jesus had told him would happen had happened. He would relive that moment many times.

So what is the evidence against Peter? He did deny his Master three times, that is clear. What we need to ask ourselves is, why? Was it pure cowardice? Was he frightened to death, afraid for his own skin? Maybe he was. Or could it be that, like many a person in a resistance movement or secret army, he was playing a part so as to remain at liberty, to be free to act on his Master's behalf if he had a chance? Here he was, as near as he possibly could be to Jesus—and where was his sword, the one he had used to cut off the servant's ear? Could it have been under his garment, ready to be used again should he be needed to come to his Master's aid?

You may come to the conclusion that Peter was a coward, that he was all bluff and that when it came to the test he failed miserably. You could point to the stories of many heroic Christian martyrs who went to their death because they would not deny they belonged to Jesus. You could tell me of those who languish in prison today because they have bravely been willing to 'stand up and be counted'. All this is true. But before you brand Peter a coward as he stood by that fire surrounded by danger, remember what Peter became later. Think, too—did his experience of failure make him a better man? Did it bring him into a closer relationship with Jesus? Did it enable him to be a more effective leader? Did it enable him to die a martyr's death with triumph? I believe the answer to all these questions is 'Yes'.

Perhaps we only get to know ourselves as we are when we are complete and utter failures—when we come to the end of ourselves, of our own abilities, of our own strength, of our own pride, and we are proved wrong. When we come to that point, and we realize to our horror and our shame just what we really are, then we can begin to grow up, to be of use to our Lord and Master.

I find failure hard to cope with, particularly my own. I like to 'win 'em all'. My own personal make-up is of a fighter who has the confidence (often very misplaced!) that I can cope on my own, can succeed where others have failed. I hold to the philosophy that 'it will be all right on the night'. There are times when I cry bitterly because I am a complete and utter failure. I fail my Lord, my loved ones and friends. I fail myself—and that is the hardest thing in the world to admit and come to terms with. In one way, I never come to terms with defeat and failure, but I can look at Peter and thank God for him. Thank God that he allowed his story to be recorded, 'warts and all'.

Peter hit the very bottom; he also hit the heights! The bottom is not a pleasant thing to hit—it hurts! I take heart from some words of Paul. There was a man who rejoiced in his own strength and power! Yet he could say this about the tough times, about the weakness he had to endure and experience:

> I prayed to the Lord about this and asked him to take it away. But his answer was: 'My grace is all you need, for my power is strongest when you are weak.' I am most happy, then, to be proud of my weaknesses, in order to feel the protection of Christ's power over me.

**2 Corinthians 12:8–9**

While Peter was experiencing weakness, another man was gloating over his own strength. That man was Annas, a very nasty piece of work altogether. He was the former high priest, father-in-law of the one in office, Caiaphas, but still holding the reins and still using that office to feather his own nest. Annas was a man who had made his money from temple business, exploiting the pilgrims. He hated Jesus, for Jesus had shown him up when he had cleared out Annas' rotten business from the house of God. Jesus was bad news for Annas—but not for much longer. Now Annas had Jesus. He called the tune.

Annas had his moment of triumph—or so he thought. He tried to look in command, blusteringly impressive; and yet Jesus simply and calmly put the ball right back in his court: 'I have always spoken publicly; I have never done anything in secret.'

Annas could not deny this fact. Jesus had a public ministry. He wasn't going to say anything different now from what he had always said. As he stood before Annas, he was the one who stood in judgment in his holiness and integrity. He stood as a challenge. Annas stood before Jesus as a cheat, one who had defamed his calling. He would be known for ever as such. He was an absolute failure as a man and as a priest—but the tragedy was, he didn't recognize that fact. He thought he was the tops, when he was actually the rock bottom.

We do well to look at Annas' life and then at our own, especially those of us who are marked as having the authority of God, as ministers and as those in leadership positions. How do we use our authority? Is it for God, or for our own advancement and to enhance our personal image?

It is so easy to pass judgment on others, on those we consider failures. How are we judged by the one we profess to serve? What will be the verdict passed on us by him? It is his verdict that matters, for it decides our ultimate destiny.

# CHAPTER 17

# 'He suffered under Pontius Pilate'

## JOHN 18:28—19:16

I was brought up in a church school in the days when religious instruction was seen as of primary importance and 'learning by heart' was the main method used. At the time, it seemed a bit—or a lot—of a bore, learning Collects and huge chunks of the Bible, reciting psalms and singing hymns. Now I thank God for that grounding in the Christian faith. It didn't make me a Christian, but it did enable me to acquire a mine of information in which to delve to discover what the faith was all about. And when I did come to a personal knowledge of Jesus Christ, the knowledge stored up in my mind was gloriously translated and became real for me.

Yet some of the things I learned by heart all those years ago were a problem to me at the time, not least because some words to a child can sound very much like another, with a totally different meaning. We may laugh at 'Harold be thy name', but to a child the name 'Harold' makes sense, where 'hallowed' is quite beyond them. One of the names that confused me for several years was Pontius Pilate. We solemnly recited the Creed at school, and I obediently said with all the others, '...suffered under Pontius Pirate'. You can imagine the picture in my mind: to me he was a cross between Long John Silver and Errol Flynn—as I said, it was a long time ago, and I was a very avid cinema-goer!

Pontius Pilate was the Roman governor, and more of a pirate than a diplomat. He had no sympathy for, or understanding of, the Jews, and rubbed them up the wrong way time after time. He never sought to make friends of them. I suppose he despised them. They were not worth anything to him except to be used in the interests of Rome and to make his own life easy. He did not want trouble, so any sign of it was firmly and brutally squashed. He also had a way of 'putting his foot in it' through tactless actions.

This was no way to govern; he was a bad choice, and complaints were laid against him to the Emperor Tiberius. The Emperor was not pleased; he did not want to be involved with the stupid mistakes of a governor, so Pilate was warned to keep the peace—or else! His position, like many others who have served as government ministers, was shaky to say the least. It was not in his interests for complaints against him to come to the Emperor's ears again. He knew that to play along with the Jews would best serve his own purposes, even though personally he had no time for them and did not understand their religious history, traditions and culture.

When Jesus was brought to him for sentence, Pilate must have groaned, 'More trouble!' It was just what he wanted to avoid; but the Jewish authorities were determined that he should make the decision that would send Jesus to his death. In the words of today, they 'made the bullets for him to fire'. Pilate wanted the Jews to take the decision. They retorted that they were not allowed to make such a decision; only the governor could do that—which was true. So Pilate began to play a game with the Jews—verbal chess, you could describe it, with Jesus as the pawn.

He talked with Jesus, questioned him, hoping that Jesus would condemn himself. But he found that Jesus was challenging him in a totally new way. Pilate was beginning to realize that Jesus was no ordinary prisoner, no mere political upstart, but someone who was innocent of the charges brought against him, yet who was a threat to him by his very innocence. Jesus claimed to speak the truth—but the world-weary Pilate, so used to deceiving and being de-ceived, had no place in his life for truth. 'And what is truth?' Pilate asked the question disparagingly. The answer stood before him—the one who was 'the way, the truth and the life'. Perhaps there was something in Pilate—behind his purpose-built defences, his seeming self-sufficiency—that craved for truth, for something that made sense of life. Was it as he spoke those words, 'And what is truth?' that he already sensed that the answer lay in the prisoner standing before him? He may not have understood the Jews and their ways; their religion was of no interest to him, he had no time for such things; he was the Emperor's man. But yet...?

William Barclay, in his commentary on John's Gospel (The Saint Andrew Press, 1955), says this:

*It was not in cynical humour that Pilate asked this question; nor was it the question of a man who did not care. Here is the chink in Pilate's armour. He asked the question wistfully and wearily. Pilate by this world's standards was a successful man. He had come almost to the top of the Roman civil service; he was governor-general of a Roman province; but there was something missing. Here in the presence of this simple, disturbing, hated Galilean, Pilate felt that for him the truth was still a mystery— and that now he had got himself into a situation where there was no chance to learn it. It may be Pilate jested, but it was the jest of despair.*

Pilate still had the chance to be somebody, a real man. He was face to face with Jesus. He could have held out his hand, could have discovered for himself the truth, God's truth. He could have had a new life, could have found the peace he longed for. But there was a price to pay; he had to surrender to the one who was his prisoner. Trying to play for time, he told the waiting crowd that he could find no reason to condemn Jesus, and as the custom was to set free a prisoner at Passover time, would they accept 'the King of the Jews'?—for in his own mind Pilate knew that Jesus was a king. There was no escape for Pilate that way. The crowd were out for blood, the blood of Jesus. So they screamed their demands even louder: 'Let the bandit called Barabbas be set free.' For Barabbas they chose life—but Jesus must die.

Pilate bowed to their request and released Barabbas, then turned his attention again to Jesus. What was he to do with him? The crowd wanted blood—they would have it! Maybe if they saw a bleeding and battered Jesus, they would be satisfied and not go on to demand the ultimate blood-letting. Maybe they would be content to see him bloodied and humiliated. So Pilate handed Jesus over to the soldiers for punishment in the barbaric manner meted out to those who upset the well-oiled wheels of government. Jesus was a nuisance, whether he was innocent or not. He had proved an embarrassment, he needed to be taught a lesson. Maybe it would deter other would-be kings.

The treatment meted out to Jesus was in no way unique. It happened then and it happens today, to many an innocent man or woman caught up in political tension, civil unrest, the clash between people of different colours and ideologies. The authorities think they have let them off lightly if they 'give them a good hiding' and release them—at least they are alive. Some are not so fortunate; their bodies are found mutilated and battered, often miles away from the point of arrest. Many others are never seen again after the arrest—innocent men and women who have been unfortunate enough to be caught up in the power struggles of others. And we do not have to look as far as Chile or South Africa—it happens much nearer home.

So Jesus experienced what many a political prisoner experiences today—the beating, the horseplay of the brutal soldiers who find their entertainment in humiliating a fellow human being, putting him through the farce of mock homage.

Their job done, they bring him back to Pilate. What does Pilate think as he views Jesus? Do his words spoken earlier to the prisoner, 'And what is truth?' stick in his throat and heart? Is he ashamed of the depths to which he and his fellow Romans have sunk? Does he feel pity for Jesus? At any rate he goes out to the Jewish crowd who are waiting for the verdict and again tells them he has no reason to condemn Jesus; there is no case to answer. Then he brings Jesus to them. 'Look, here is the man!' The translation of the words he used is more like, 'Look at this poor fellow.' You would have thought the sight of Jesus, of any man, in that state would have brought them to their senses. You could have hoped there would have even been pity, a feeling of guilt, a turning away in shame. But no, like a pack of wolves with blood in their nostrils they are eager to be in for the final destruction. 'Crucify, crucify!' is their hysterical response to the sight of Jesus.

Pilate stands his ground, and again tells them he has no reason to find Jesus guilty; there is no evidence. 'We have a law that says he ought to die because he claimed to be the Son of God,' insist the crowd. Pilate is scared stiff; he realizes he is out of his depth, he cannot cope with the situation. Jesus frightens him more than the crowd. Pilate can cope with hatred, he has seen it all before. He cannot cope with goodness, with innocence, with the truth; for if Jesus is the Son of God…?

Now even the prisoner remains silent before him. There are no words of explanation, no plea for mercy; he says nothing. But he does not need to speak. Pilate knows in his heart that this man should not die. He pleads with Jesus to answer, reminding Jesus that he has the power of life and death over him by virtue of his office as governor. But Jesus' reply sends the shivers down his spine, for Jesus reminds Pilate that he has power only because God has given it to him—what an awesome responsibility!

Pilate knows clearly what he should do, so he tries to reason with the crowd. But they, realizing his weakness, play their trump card: 'If you set him free, that means that you are not the Emperor's friend!' It is blackmail now, and Pilate knows it. They have hit him where it hurts. He knows that his own career, his own life, are finished unless he goes against his better judgment. And so he gives in to the mob.

Pilate knows that Jesus is King, for he has proved it without a doubt, and yet he has to die. 'Here is your king,' says Pilate; but there is no shout of acclamation, no trumpet sounds, no royal salute—only the insistent shouts of 'Crucify!' Pilate, in mocking tone, puts the question to which he already has the answer. 'Do you want me to crucify your king?' But the chief priests, gleefully knowing they have won the day, negate the fundamental heart of their faith: 'The only king we have is the Emperor!' They deny their God whom they claim to worship. They have won the day, but they have lost everything. They have bowed to Rome; they have betrayed their prophets, priests and kings, and God himself. The chosen people have chosen to go the way of the world; they have deposed the everlasting God for an earthly pagan despot in acknowledging the Emperor as their king.

Professor Leon Morris, in *The Gospel According to John*, says this of them: 'Thus he (Pilate) extracted from them the last affirmation they would normally be willing to make. They spoke in terms of cynical expediency. But they expressed the real truth.' They had no king but the dictate of a foreign power, they had sunk to that point, by choice. They had turned their back on God's gift; soon they would see him nailed down and launched up into the sky for all to see. What sort of a king was that? For them, even a foreign heathen power was to be preferred! And Pilate? He had done his best in a way; he had tried to save Jesus, he had done more than many another would have done. But pride and fear won the day; his job and his skin mattered most.

The events of that day are re-enacted over and over again. The names, the places and the dates are different, but the story is the same. There are those who 'dot the i's and cross the t's', who make sure they observe the religious niceties, play their part in ceremonials, do not defile their bodies by entering into forbidden territory; and yet blaspheme and pollute by their greed and anger, their pettiness, their craving for power. There are those who know what they should be, what they should do; they half-heartedly point in the right direction but waver; they are afraid to do wrong but afraid to do right. What finally decides them is not truth but expediency. They take the easy way out. They cannot pay the price of truth.

Pilate could have saved Jesus. He had the power, but he wasn't prepared to use it to save him, wasn't prepared to face the consequences from 'on high'. There are many Pilates today who sit in the seats of power, who are called to make judgments and pass sentence, and they do so influenced by public demand, political pressure, personal preference and their own pride and fears. Look around the world—there they sit, there they pontificate—and watch how they fall!

There's a bit of Pilate in me. I do my best, make my points, but then when things get nasty I draw back. And there are times when, out of fear of what people will think of me, or pride in what I think I am, I capitulate. I know, of course, in my heart of hearts, when I have taken the coward's way out and let selfishness and pride win the day. Sometimes I am able to redress the balance, to confess or apologize; but sadly, most times I just let it go, and hope no one will remember.

Did Pilate think anyone would remember what happened that day? After all, it was just one event among many. Just another poor wretch who opened his mouth too much, who didn't watch his manners, got on the wrong side of the powers that be, and who was made a public example. Men on crosses were ten-a-penny in his day; life had always been cheap. Who would remember Jesus of Nazareth, the wandering preacher, the chap who worked miracles, who ruffled the feathers of the local religious leaders? Who would remember him, his life or his death, and the people who were part of both? It would all die down in time. It always did—didn't it?

Poor Pilate, for ever to be known as the one who sent Jesus to his death, who turned him over for execution! He did not know that two thousand years later people would still speak his name as they stood to affirm the Lordship of Jesus Christ—the King who 'suffered under Pontius Pilate, was crucified, died and was buried...' It is easy to be wise after the event, isn't it?

Will anyone remember my cowardice, my sitting on the fence, my misplaced pride? I have the awful feeling and the chilling assurance within me that someone will, unless I do something about it—now.

CHAPTER 18

# *He is the King*

## JOHN 19:17–24

Pilate had tried to save Jesus. He had done his best, but his best had not been good enough. The chief priests with their theological arguments and their veiled threats, the crowd getting larger and nastier by the minute, had finally won, and Pilate handed Jesus over to them. It was just a matter of time before he would be nailed to the cross, for there would be no last-minute change of heart or reprieve.

Now the routine of execution begins, with the condemned man carrying his own execution block. Could human beings stoop so low as to make a man carry the instrument of his own death? But there is nothing new under the sun. How often we read of men and women being made to dig their own graves before being killed, adding yet another cruel twist to the occasion, another sadistic turn of the screw to the cold, calculating cruelty of humankind.

So Jesus staggers along, battered and bleeding, with the cross on his back, going the way many a man has gone before him, and many a man after. Mark's Gospel records that Jesus fell under the weight of the cross and a passer-by was pressganged into carrying it for him; but Jesus was made to carry it himself for most of the way, at any rate. In the jeering, howling crowd that lined the route, were there any who, as Pilate had done, pointed to Jesus and said, 'Look at the poor fellow'? I feel sure there would have been—maybe among those who had been healed or helped by Jesus, who had known the touch of his hand, his words of comfort and assurance in their pain and despair. Those who had felt that Jesus was their hope and their future now saw the sorry spectacle of him in defeat, a prisoner on his way to death. Perhaps, too, there were those who knew nothing of him but who felt sorry for 'the poor fellow', and who turned away shuddering to think of the pain he would have to endure before death finally brought him release.

Pilate may have lost his battle for the life of Jesus but he had one last card which he could and did play. A notice was customarily affixed to declare the name and the crime of each person to be executed. This would be publicly displayed as the prisoner made his way to the place of execution, so that all would see who he was and what crime he had committed. It could act as a useful deterrent, an awful warning to any who may have felt inclined to commit another such offence. Finally it would be fixed on the cross as a macabre headboard. Pilate wrote the inscription for Jesus; it was his chance to say the last word on Jesus, and so he wrote, 'Jesus of Nazareth, the King of the Jews'. To make sure everyone could read and understand it, he deliberately wrote it in the three great languages commonly in use: Hebrew, Latin and Greek.

The chief priests were furious. They demanded that Pilate amend it to read, 'This man *said*, "I am the King of the Jews."' Pilate refused to alter what he had written; at last he dug his heels in. He had been beaten by the Jews in the battle over Jesus, when they used their trump card against him by declaring their allegiance to Rome. So let them taste the power of Rome. Pilate declared his judgment on Jesus and let the world see it: 'What I have written stays written.'

You could say that what Pilate did was 'too little, too late'. Maybe he did it out of annoyance, determined to rub the noses of the priests in the dirt they had descended to; he wanted to humiliate them as they had humiliated him. I would like to think that Pilate also did it for Jesus, because Jesus had convinced him of his right to the title. Yes, maybe it was 'too little, too late', but it was better than nothing; it was an acknowledgment of the truth.

Too little, too late! Do you ever feel as I do, that the little we could do is not worth doing because it is too late? What use is an afterthought, a post-event protest? Those occasions when we lack the guts to do anything about a situation until the opportunity has passed and time has run out—what is the use of protesting then, after it has happened? I don't believe action is ever wasted. We may have to eat humble pie ourselves, because our very protesting after the event shows us up as cowards, people who had not got the courage of their own convictions at the time it really mattered. Yet we should respond to the voice of conscience and do the little we can, even in retrospect—for who knows what it may accomplish?

Pilate's weakness was recorded for all time; but so was his

protest, his stand for Jesus. So I take heart from that, for it shows that the belated token stand—yes, even yours and mine—can be used to bring glory to God, and knowing that should encourage us even when all seems lost through our own weakness.

That sign must have infuriated the Jews. There it was for all to see and read and ponder on. It was the verdict of Rome on Jesus of Nazareth. It still stands for all the world to see, to read and to ponder on.

For the soldiers who carried out the execution, it would make little difference who the man on the cross was. He was just another job, all part of a day's work; they were the ones on duty at the time, so they carried out the execution. They were not personally involved. They didn't understand the issue. They were only concerned to get the assignment over and divide the spoils between them, the belongings of the executed man which were the perks of their trade. They were quite indifferent to the sufferings, only concerned for their share of what was to be had. So there they were, playing a game as Jesus died. Callous, brutal, hard men, professional soldiers, just doing their duty, obeying orders; feelings did not enter into it.

The other Gospel accounts record that the officer on duty was affected. He must have attended many crucifixions as duty officer, but he saw something different in this man going to his death. He was convinced of his innocence. And more than that, he was sure that Jesus was a good man; could it even be possible that this man was the Son of God? He watched him die and came to his conclusion, and voiced it.

The Roman officer looked and saw who Jesus really was; he recognized God on the cross. Jesus would not have looked like a god hanging there; he would have looked 'a poor fellow'. But the Roman saw what others missed, saw the divine clothed in battered, bleeding, dying human flesh.

In the chapel of the Trinity and All Saints College in Horsforth in Leeds, there is a crucifix. It dominates that chapel, and as soon as you enter, your eyes are drawn to it. I have seen it many times, and each time it speaks to me afresh of Jesus who suffered and died for me, who gave his life in its prime for me. It makes me want to weep, for I realize that it is my sin that put Jesus on the cross, just as much as if I had personally hammered in the nails. But it also speaks to me of the voluntary nature of the suffering. Jesus died because he loved men and women so much—men and women of all generations, including me. For it was love that held him there, not the nails of men.

In 1986, Yorkshire Television recorded a service in that chapel. It was specially for people who suffered from communication disorders, their families and friends and those who cared for them. As the Anglican Adviser to Yorkshire Television, I spent a great deal of time in the chapel as preparations were made and rehearsals went on, and so I was able to look at that particular cross from many angles. I found that time a very moving experience, particularly in the context of the service we were recording.

The preacher at the service was Canon Jim Richardson, then Vicar of Leeds, and he too, in his sermon, pointed to that cross, saying with reference to suffering and pain:

> *Isn't that the message of this chapel crucifix? The suffering Christ who in his own body reveals to us the true nature of God. Not remote and unreal, but Love itself. But note the rebellion too. The body is arched away from the cross. It is straining upwards. The sigh for humanity is there, but it anticipates the resurrection, and the victory over sin, evil and death in all their forms. Christ reigns on that tree!*

Yes—'King of kings and Lord of lords... He shall reign for ever and ever.' But there are still those who are indifferent, those who reject him, those who hate him. There are still those who play games and ignore him. That is their choice. There are also those who look and see and begin to understand what he is all about, and who go on to discover for themselves the glorious truth written in flesh on the tree.

Jesus was lifted up, as he said he would be. He drew, and still draws, men and women to meet him, to follow him. But beware before you make your decision, for he said this: 'If anyone wants to come with me, he must forget self, carry his cross and follow me.'

Look at the cross—that is the price of love. If you follow the one who died on the cross, it could cost you your life too. Think carefully, very carefully, before you decide.

# CHAPTER 19

# Love is stronger than death

## JOHN 19:25–37

It was no place for them to be, watching an execution; particularly one like this. For death was not to come swiftly—with the flash of a blade, the violent pull on the end of a rope or the sickening thud of a club—but as the result of a slow, agonizing, barbaric form of torture. The atmosphere was horrendous for anyone with an ounce of feeling in them. Think of that scene—three men being publicly executed, the crowd seeing it as frightening entertainment, some jeering and shouting in triumph, gloating over those who had caused them trouble, and who now would trouble them no more. The soldiers, in their rough, callous way, keeping order and making sure that everything went according to plan, with military precision. Think too of the heat, the flies, the noise, the dust and the smell.

It was no place for anyone to be who cared for any of those poor wretches being executed. Certainly no place for a woman! Much better if they were kept well away. It was bad enough to know what was happening, but actually seeing it—it could turn their minds. They could always visit the grave afterwards, take some flowers, have someone around to comfort them in the peace and quiet; but to be at the actual execution—no.

It was no place for them to be, but the only place they could be; it was the place of love. What a sad little group! There was Jesus' mother, Mary, and her sister; Mary, the wife of Clopas (one ancient tradition says that Clopas was the brother of Joseph, so that would make her the sister-in-law of Mary, Jesus' mother); and the fourth woman, Mary Magdalene, who had once been healed by Jesus. With the quartet of sorrowing women was John, the one disciple brave enough to come so close to the scene. John bore a double burden, that of his own deep sorrow and also the task of comforting and supporting those weeping women. It says a lot about John to know that he was there, that he was the one who stood by the women as well as by Jesus. He must have been a tremendous support to their dreadful ordeal.

How did Jesus feel as he looked down from the cross on that little group of people, who loved him so much that they were willing to undergo the agony of being there, unable to do anything but stand by him and love him with all their hearts? Jesus saw his heartbroken mother and he saw his friend. He said to his mother, of John, 'He is your son'; and to John, as he entrusted his mother to him, 'She is your mother.' He brought them into a special relationship with each other, so that they could comfort one another, care for each other; they would be good for one another in the days that lay ahead.

Jesus knew the importance of human relationships. He fully understood loneliness, 'being left'. On the cross he experienced terrible loneliness; he felt forsaken, even by his Father. He knew what it was like. He went through it.

Perhaps the greatest burden of bereavement for anyone is that of 'being left'; feeling totally alone, with no one to share things with, no one to care deeply about them. As I have been writing this I have been talking to a man who has, in the space of a few months, lost his wife, his son and daughter-in-law. 'I live on my own,' he told me. 'It's awful. I keep picking up things that belonged to them, and they've gone, and I'm all on my own, and nobody knows what it's like.'

Nobody knows what it's like—except someone who has gone through it. And Jesus has gone through it. He does know. He does care. The song called 'The Streets of London' includes the words: 'All the lonely people, where do they all come from?' So many lonely people—especially those who have been bereaved, who have lost the one who meant everything to them, and life now seems empty and hollow.

Jesus brought together two desperately lonely and sad people, his mother and John. I believe he wants to bring the lonely and sad together today. I look around the church and see the folk who live alone, who sit alone, who are alone. They need someone, they need each other. Perhaps we should remember what Jesus did when he introduced John and his mother into a new and special relationship. They both knew and loved him; he was their common bond. So why are there so many lonely and isolated

Christians? Perhaps you are one. Could it be that Jesus is asking you to be a mother, or a son, or a special friend to someone in the same position? Would you be brave enough, caring enough, to make the first move—for his sake?

Jesus knew that his mother would be well cared for. He knew now that his friend had a mother to love and be loved by. As a son and as a friend, he had lovingly cared for them to the end. He had looked to their future and made provision for them. What an example of love! In all his desperate suffering, he was concerned for those he loved and who loved him.

When I am in pain, worried or fearful, my thoughts are entirely self-centred. I can only see me and my troubles. I want the world to revolve around me. When I am hurt by someone else, my only concern is for myself. I cannot see further than Margaret Cundiff. Yet I read of the care Jesus took of others when he was hanging from the cross, when he was suffering so terribly because of the hatred and rottenness of those who had put him there. He was still concerned, still loving, still planning for the good of other people. It makes me hang my head in shame at my own selfishness and lack of love and concern; at the 'I' that is so uppermost in my mind that it often obliterates the crying needs of others.

Jesus suffered—really suffered—in every part of him. How thirsty he must have been. How much he longed for just a taste of something cool on his parched lips; and his cry, 'I am thirsty' was met with a wet sponge full of cheap wine, raised to his lips in a last act of kindness. Maybe one of the soldiers felt sorry for him, and in a rough and ready manner did what he could for 'that poor fellow'. The one who did that act is unknown to us, but known to Jesus, appreciated for ever. It was just a small act. Probably the one who did it never gave it another thought, and would have been astonished to know that his act would be remembered two thousand years on, and will be remembered as long as time lasts. 'Little things mean a lot,' says the old song. Yes, they do; and we are all capable of little acts of kindness, the response to need, 'putting ourselves out'.

I was hurrying along the road one afternoon, intent on getting to the bank before it closed, when an old lady touched my arm and said, 'Are you going across the road?' 'No,' I replied, and was about to rush on, when she said very wistfully, 'Only I can't see very well and I'm frightened of the traffic.' I must admit that part of me still wanted to rush on, but I turned round, got hold of her arm and slowly we walked to the crossing, waited and went across. As we made it to the other side, she turned and smiled at me. 'God bless you, luv,' she said. I felt a real heel!

My response of caring had not been immediate or spontaneous, but I was so glad she gave me a second chance to do what I knew I should—and the bank was still open when I got there! Cheap wine on a sponge meant so much to Jesus. Our small, simple acts of kindness mean so much to those around who are in need of maybe just a hand, a smile, a lift, a word.

Jesus received that gift of a drink, then he 'bowed his head and died'. Luke records that he said, 'Father! In your hands I place my spirit!' (Luke 23:46). It was the prayer every Jewish child said on going to bed. Jesus died like a child going to sleep, secure in the love of his Father, with perfect trust and confidence as he fell asleep. What better words to be on our lips as we put our head on the pillow each night? What better words to be on our lips and in our hearts as we close our eyes, even for the last time?

Jesus was dead—but the soldier made doubly sure by plunging his spear into his side. Jesus was dead all right—very dead. The other two men who had been crucified may have shown some signs of being still alive, so their legs were smashed to finish them off. Time was now short before the Sabbath day, and as the Sabbath day was holy, the Jews did not want bodies hanging about. Get rid of them, get them out of the way, forget what had happened; the Sabbath must not be disturbed.

'Out of sight, out of mind.' The crowd would disperse, to go home and get ready for the Sabbath. The soldiers would tidy up and report back to barracks, then go off to enjoy themselves with their families, meeting their girlfriends, getting drunk, sleeping it off—whatever soldiers find to do when they have finished their duties. Already the hours on duty would be receding from their memories, and tomorrow was another day.

Yes, life goes on, even after a death; even after many deaths. Time goes relentlessly on: the minutes, the hours, the days, the years. 'Time, like an ever rolling sea, bears all its sons away.' It was just another crucifixion day, just another three men thrust into eternity, a very ordinary day really, just like any other. Those who lived through that day would not know that for ever that day would have a special name—it would be called 'Good Friday'. 'Good' Friday? Not much good about it, was there? It was a bleak, bad, horrible day. For some it was the worst day of their lives; for others a day of revenge and satisfaction which had brought the worst out in them. But it was 'Good Friday' for all who would look to the one who hung on the cross—the man in the middle—and put their trust in him.

> *He died that we might be forgiven,*
> *He died to make us good,*
> *That we might go at last to heaven*
> *Saved by his precious blood.*

**C.F. Alexander (1818–95)**

He did that, on Good Friday, and he did it for you and for me. But what effect has it on us? We know the story so well—so how real is it for you now?

At our Family Service at Easter time, a group of our church members were portraying in mime the death of Jesus. A young man, Jonathan, was playing the part of Jesus. The blows were aimed at him as he was hoisted roughly on to a platform at the front of the church. His arms were stretched out, the make-believe nails hammered in. It was a most moving portrayal of the crucifixion; we were all deeply impressed by it. But of course, we knew the story; we knew what was happening.

From my stall, I could see not only the drama but the rapt expressions on the faces of the congregation, and I thought, 'We must do this more often, it really holds their attention.' Then suddenly an agonized scream rang through the quiet church, followed by uncontrollable crying. It went through me, as I am sure it did through every person in the church. It came from a very small person, only a year old, who had been watching wide-eyed from the safety of a comfortable pair of knees. She was only a baby; she did not know the story, she was too young to understand. So why was she so distressed? Why was her pain so real? It was quite simple. Jonathan, who was playing the part of Jesus, was her daddy. All she knew was that Daddy was being hurt; she could do nothing to help him, she could not even get to him. She could only express her feelings in desperate crying and screaming. It took a long time before Rachel was pacified that morning, but later, cradled in her father's arms, she eventually allowed herself to be comforted, and knew that everything was all right again.

Perhaps that morning all of us in the church learned something very important. We learned it not by our heads, intellectually accepting the suffering and death of Jesus, but through the crying of a child responding to her father's pain; and through seeing, too, the real anguish on that young father's face as he played out his part while his daughter cried. It was not just good acting, it was real, for he could do nothing to relieve his child's distress until his part had been played out.

The death of Jesus is so familiar that maybe we have lost something by its very familiarity. It took a child's scream and a young father's pained face to remind me of what 'Good Friday' was really about. It brought me afresh to look at the cross and to look at myself, and to re-echo the words written by Isaac Watts (1674–1748):

*Were the whole realm of nature mine,*
*That were an offering far too small;*
*Love so amazing, so divine,*
*Demands my life, my soul, my all!*

# CHAPTER 20

# Now he's dead and gone

## JOHN 19:38—20:10

'When is the funeral?' That is one of the first questions we ask when we receive the news of the death of a relative or friend. We want to show our respect and love by being there, sending flowers, getting in touch with the family. The funeral arrangements are made by the next of kin, the one closest to the person who has died. That person is the one who has to go to the Registrar with the doctor's certificate and register the death to obtain a death certificate, so that the funeral can then take place. The next of kin has to make all the arrangements with the funeral director. There are friends to be contacted, usually the bank and the insurance companies to be informed; there is so much to be done within the space of a very short time. But there is often another member of the family, a close friend, who will help with all the running around and be an arm to lean on while the necessary but very emotional details have to be dealt with.

So what would happen to the body of Jesus? Would anyone be allowed to have it? After all, Jesus had been put to death by the authorities; it was up to them to decide about the disposal of the body—they could do with it what they willed. It was likely that they would want to oversee the arrangements, particularly as Jesus had made some very extravagant claims about rising from the dead. It could be that his friends would fabricate some story about his coming back to life—so the authorities would want a very close watch put on his body, certainly until all the interest in Jesus had died down.

Who was the next of kin? Surely it was Jesus' mother, or one of his brothers, or even one of his close friends, one of those who had been his companions during the last three years. Yet it was none of them but Joseph of Arimathea who went to Pilate and asked for the body. An interesting character, was Joseph. He was rich and influential, a member of the Council called the Sanhedrin that had tried Jesus; but he had not agreed with either the way they had gone about the trial or the decision they had come to. Luke tells us, 'He was a good and honourable man, who was waiting for the coming of the Kingdom of God' (Luke 23:50–51).

He spoke out on behalf of Jesus, but would not take a stand as one of his followers, for he was afraid of his fellow councillors. So he became a secret follower, not prepared to nail his colours to the mast and take the risk of losing his position, even though he believed Jesus was right.

Now Jesus was dead, so maybe it was as well that Joseph had not declared himself as a follower; he could have lost everything and been left with nothing. Yet he boldly went and asked for the body, acting as 'next of kin', you could say. He found the courage now which he had lacked before. How do you explain that?

He was joined by fellow member of the Sanhedrin, Nicodemus, who provided all the spices for the anointing of Jesus' body and assisted Joseph with the preparation and the burial. Nicodemus was a fascinating character. Early on in Jesus' ministry, he had come at night to talk with him about spiritual issues; he wanted to find out the truth, and was willing to listen to the wandering preacher called Jesus. He wasn't too proud to ask, but he was too timid to ask publicly. The conversation between them has been the means of countless people coming into faith, and perhaps one of the best-loved verses in the Bible is 'God loved the world so much that he gave his only Son, so that everyone who believes in him may not die but have eternal life' (John 3:16). It has been preached on and written about, times without number. It has been set to music in every style from the classics to pop and rock, and has been the word of assurance to many a timid soul who has come wanting to know for sure that they could really have a new start.

Now Nicodemus saw the dead and battered body of Jesus and did what he could to afford him a dignified burial. Joseph and Nicodemus—two men who, if they had spoken out, if they had been brave, if they had been true to their convictions, could have saved Jesus. How did they feel as they saw his body, as they anointed him and wrapped him in the grave clothes? What did they say? What could they say?

We cannot stand in judgment on those two men unless we can put our hand on our heart and say we have never failed in our witness, never let an opportunity go by to share Jesus, never been at all reticent in going into 'the lion's den'. I look into my own heart and have to confess that I have failed to speak out; I have been too concerned for my own position, my own standing. I have been in gatherings where 'simple faith' has been scorned, where those who claim to have been 'converted' or 'born again' have been regarded with amusement and as suspect candidates for any high office. And there have been times when I have kept quiet. Oh yes, I was content to scurry back home and be known there as a 'born-again, converted, Bible-believing Christian'—but not in some sophisticated, high-powered centres of discussion and learning. I do not want to appear as 'the country cousin', or 'just a good simple woman'—not me! So I keep quiet, or lamely make some half-hearted comment.

Joseph and Nicodemus were the bravest of the brave, heroes of the faith compared with me—and perhaps with you, too! They were brave when all seemed lost—or could it have been that those last days of Jesus, including his death, had finally convinced them, against all the odds, against all human reasoning, that this Jesus was the Son of God, in spite of his seeming defeat? As they tenderly and reverently laid his body to rest, was there within them the seed of hope that this was not the last they would see or hear of Jesus? As the stone was rolled against the entrance to the tomb, did they really think it was the end? What was in their minds as they left the scene? There was no doubt that the cross was already acting as a symbol of triumph rather than failure, for two silent men had now found their voices and their courage, the strength to act, the power to witness; but little did they know then what was to follow. All they knew was that they had done what they knew they had to do. And perhaps that is what we are called to do, day by day—to do what we know we should do, and do it for him.

Next morning a sorrowing woman, Mary Magdalene, came to visit the grave. Brave woman! She had stood by the cross with that small, devoted and devastated group of people, witnessing the terrible events, the desolation, the darkness of death. She loved Jesus so much. He had given her a new life, she would have given it gladly for him; and now he was dead and all she could do was pay her last respects. She must have been totally exhausted, both physically and mentally; yet she came in the darkness of the early morning to be near Jesus. So much for the argument of women being the weaker sex, not being able to cope with the traumas and tragic events of life like men can! Woman may be weaker physically, but because of their capacity to love so deeply and intently, they can and often do overcome seemingly impossible odds through that power of love, finding a strength beyond their own.

Mary came to the tomb—and what she saw when she arrived must almost have finished her. It was the final blow: the stone at the entrance had been removed, the body was gone. And so, shocked and distraught, she ran to tell Peter and John the dreadful news. It must have seemed to her the end of the world—her world. Surely nothing could be worse than what had happened now! There was no depth below this. It was the end.

There are times, maybe, when we think we have reached the end of our tether and will snap altogether; times when there is no hope, no help. I remember one Sunday morning when Trevor, a Methodist minister, was preaching at one of the united services we hold from time to time in Selby. In the course of his sermon he said, 'When you think you are at the end of your tether, remember who holds the other end.' It has stuck in my mind ever since. There have been many occasions when I have remembered that saying, and it has given me renewed hope and strength.

I remember that story for another reason also, because although Trevor did not realize it, there was a man in the congregation that morning who was at the end of his tether. He was at breaking point; he had come to the end of his resources; he was on the verge of a breakdown. And those words, 'When you think you are at the end of your tether, remember who holds the other end', came to him as a word from the Lord and pulled him back from the edge, from despair, from giving up. He knew again the joy and assurance of being held fast and secure by 'the one who holds the other end'. That morning he made a new start, with a new confidence which has not left him or let him go.

Mary was at the end of her tether. My friend in church that morning was at the end of his. I've been at the end of mine many times, and no doubt so have you. But remember Jesus, the one who holds the other end, who will never let you go, who will hold you safe for all eternity; the one who was 'crucified, died and was buried', but who did not remain so. No tomb could hold him, no stone withhold him, no grave clothes restrain him, no human power defeat him—nor us, either.

# CHAPTER 21

# *But how do you know it was him?*

## JOHN 20:11–18

Some years ago, we were on a parish outing in the Yorkshire Dales. We had walked steadily uphill and finally found ourselves on a grassy stretch of flat ground, an ideal stopping-place for our picnic lunch. We had settled down to enjoy lunch, sunbathe, and rest from our strenuous walk, when we heard shouting, and saw someone running towards us. We could not make out the words properly—the runner was almost hysterical—but we quickly realized that one of our party, the vicar's small son, had fallen over the edge of a sheer drop.

We all began to scramble to our feet, James, the vicar, followed by some of the men, racing in the direction of the cliff. We were absolutely terrified, sure that Philip was dead at the bottom of the cliff. But by a miracle he had been caught up in a bush, the only bush there was, and was rescued, scratched, crying, but unhurt, his main complaint being that he had lost his sandal. He soon recovered from his ordeal; but for the rest of us it was a very frightening experience which took a long time to get over. There were many racing hearts that day, with blood pressures sky high. We shuddered to think what might have been—it was not an experience any of us would like to go through again.

As I read of Mary dashing off with the news that the tomb is empty and Jesus' body gone, as she incoherently spills out her story to Peter and John and they set off running towards the tomb, I see in my mind's eye the scene as in the Dales. I sense the absolute fear and confusion, hear the thudding of men's feet, the heavy breathing, feel the perspiration rise—born of fear and exertion. Peter goes into the tomb, and sees that it is as Mary has said—it is empty. The neatly placed grave clothes are there, but the one who had been wrapped in them has gone. John quickly joins Peter and sees for himself. They both know Mary is telling the truth, it is no delusion. The tomb is wide open to the world, Jesus is definitely not there—but where is he? Peter and John return home, no doubt to share the grim news, to ask if anyone has heard anything that might throw some light, to try to make sense of all this.

And Mary? She remains outside the tomb, glued to the spot, crying. It is the end of her world. She is unable to move, frozen by grief. Then she takes a look inside the tomb—maybe the body has been moved around but is still there; perhaps there may be some clue as to what has happened. She sees two angels, dressed in white, sitting where Jesus had been lying. They ask her why she is crying and she tells them, 'They have taken my Lord away, and I do not know where they have put him!' She is not interested in the angels, nor in awe of them; all she can think of is Jesus. She is asked a question, and gives her answer.

How would you have reacted to the sight of two angels—or even one, for that matter? How did she know they were angels? All that John records is that they were angels. Were they two of the ones who sang with joy at Jesus' birth, I wonder? What is certain is that there is a good case for angels. They are recorded for us in the Bible, they were accepted by those who wrote down the events that took place. So we can be sure that angels do exist.

There is someone else now at the tomb. He asks Mary the same question as the angels: why is she crying? And then he adds, 'Who is it that you are looking for?' Mary realizes that here is someone who might help her to find Jesus. Maybe he is the one who has moved the body. Perhaps he works in the garden. So many ideas must have gone through her head—but now she has a chance to find out what has happened, and if this man was the one who removed the body, then perhaps if he tells her where it is she can go and get it back. Brave, loving Mary! What an example of commitment to Jesus! Nothing would hold her back from her Lord; she would stand against the world for him, resist the strongest and fiercest for him. She didn't know who 'they' were, what she was up against, but she was determined to overcome anything and anyone to be reunited with Jesus. Then the man says one word, her name—'Mary'.

She knows instantly, he is no gardener. She recognizes his voice. There is no doubt who he is—he is Jesus.

This raises the questions in some people's minds. Why was it that she didn't recognize him at first? Where was he when Peter and John came? And the biggest question of all, how could she be so sure it was him? Could she have been mistaken, in such a state of shock, grief and terror that her mind played tricks and she was having hallucinations? Mary was sure enough. And now she wants to hold him, grasp him, fling her arms round him, be held by him; but he stops her from doing so. He does not allow her to hang on and keep him to herself. He has work for her to do. She is to go and tell the others he is alive; he has risen from the dead as he promised.

So she goes, this time running with joy. This time it is good news, the greatest news, the seemingly impossible news, the news Jesus' friends didn't dare think about because it was beyond their wildest hopes and dreams—'Jesus is alive!'

I hardly think that Mary would have been believed by them at first. The terrible time they had all gone through would mean they were in a complete daze; and Mary—well, she had suffered more than most. She'd seen everything, seen Jesus crucified, seen the empty tomb, seen... seen what... who? Had she really? Do you think she did meet with Jesus, or was she deluded? Was it all just wishful thinking translated into a human mirage?

I believe it was just as it says it was. You may think it was too good to be true, but surely it was too good *not* to be true! It rings true!

Once, in London, I was walking through Trafalgar Square. It was crowded with people, many of them tourists, chattering away in every language under the sun; businessmen and women were trying to push their way through, heading for the station; there was a roar and a rumble of traffic all around; and I heard a voice say, 'Margaret!' I knew, although I could not see, who it was. There was no mistaking the voice. Not that it was any louder, higher or deeper than any of the many voices around—but it was a voice I recognized, and I knew who it was by the way he spoke my name. It was an old friend whom I had not seen for a long time; certainly I had no idea he was in London that day. But I knew who it was before my eyes made him out, walking towards me smiling, his hand outstretched.

I expect you have had similar experiences. Someone has called your name, and although there may have been a hundred there with the same name, you knew it was for you, because of the tone, the inflection in the voice—you just knew!

I am sure Mary got it right, too! It was Jesus. He lovingly chose her to be the first person to meet him after his resurrection, and he called her by name. That gives me great heart! Whatever may be said for or against the ordination of women, however much discussion takes place on whether a woman is capable of being a minister, in the end it doesn't really matter. For I know there were women who stood by Jesus, even as he died; it was a woman who was the first to see him alive; it was to a woman that he gave the privilege of telling others. Whatever men or women or the Church may think about the ministry of women, Jesus himself was a great supporter and encourager of women, giving them a ministry and mission in his name.

What really matters is not the argument about men or women, or even angels, but the fact that Jesus is alive. He is risen. He is alive for ever more.

He is still meeting with people as personally as he did that day when he spoke to Mary by name. He knows each one of us by name, and if you will listen you will hear him—even at this very moment.

*Speak, Lord, in the stillness,*
*While I wait on Thee;*
*Hushed my heart to listen*
*In expectancy.*

*Fill me with the knowledge*
*Of Thy glorious will;*
*All Thine own good pleasure*
*In Thy child fulfil.*

**Emily M. Crawford (1868–1927)**

# CHAPTER 22

# Behind closed doors

## JOHN 20:19–30

Just down the road from our home is Carlton Towers, the Yorkshire home of the Duke of Norfolk. Originally built in the seventeenth century, and much rebuilt in 1820 and 1874, it is surrounded by extensive grounds, and is now open to the public at certain times of the year. While not as large or as well known as some of the other stately homes, it is attracting an increasing number of visitors, who enjoy exploring the grounds and seeing round the house, which is still very much lived in. One of the fascinating rooms upstairs houses a 'priest's hole', and the guide explains to visitors that during the time when it was an offence, punishable by law, to take part in a Roman Catholic service, or to harbour a Roman Catholic priest, this secret hideaway was used by priests visiting the house, where they could be safe from the officers of the Crown. When the premises were searched, there would be no sign of a priest or of a Mass being celebrated. Only when the officers had left, satisfied that no one illegal was in the house, would the signal be given and those behind the locked and secret door be able to breathe a sigh of relief.

Hiding behind locked and secret doors has been the fate of many throughout history, in political and religious groups. During wartime, those 'on the run' in enemy territory have sheltered behind locked doors and in hidden places, and today throughout the world there are many behind locked doors in fear of those who seek to destroy them because of the faith they hold. As I share so openly in worship and witness in this country, I thank God each time I do so for the freedom I possess, for being able to declare my faith openly, without fear. We are so fortunate in the UK. I wonder whether we are always aware of our blessings, and whether we support enough in prayer those who have to meet behind locked doors in other lands.

Men and women who have known what it is like to have had to

hide behind locked doors, and those whose experience it is today, will identify with the close friends of Jesus who 'gathered together behind locked doors, because they were afraid of the Jewish authorities'. They were desperately afraid and bewildered. They had lived through the most awful days in the history of the world. They had seen their hopes dashed, as their leader had been brutally put to death.

Jesus was dead, all right. His had been a public, very public execution. Then his body had been placed in the tomb and the heavy stone placed across it, finalizing the life and death of Jesus. Yet now that tomb was empty, the stone rolled away—but by whom? Could it have been the authorities, who would not even allow his body to rest in peace and honour? Surely they had done enough to that body, flogged, tormented and broken? Mary Magdalene had discovered the empty tomb and had come running for Peter and John, and they confirmed what she had said; but later she had arrived with the fantastic story that she had seen Jesus alive and that he had sent a message for them—but who could believe poor Mary? She had gone through so much anguish, it must have turned her brain! Grief can do that to a person, especially to a woman—such emotional creatures, women!

If only what Mary had told them could have been true! Could it possibly be true? Their hearts hoped, but their heads knew the hard facts. And yet, what was the truth? Would it ever be known? What was to become of them all now, they who had shared so much together with Jesus? They had come to love one another; they wanted to stay together; but what was the point? Anyway, surely it would be better to go away, back home, to take up the old life again, separately. If they remained together, it was likely that they would face the same fate as Jesus; they would be thought of as a band of freedom fighters. They were conspicuous as a group; separately they could, perhaps, merge into the background.

Meanwhile, there they were behind locked doors—as a group, but also as individuals, each one with his memories, his fears, his questions. Every movement, every sound, jogged them into an awareness of how much in danger they were; and deep down was the fear that they would be dragged away to suffer the same fate as Jesus—a dreadful prospect!

And then, suddenly, Jesus was there—right there with them. No ghost, no figment of their imagination; it was him all right, he showed them his wounds, and yet he was alive and well—and yes, even more alive than ever. His words, 'Peace be with you', were both a greeting and a blessing. They had heard him say those words so often; he had promised them peace, and the sight of his wounds showed them the price of peace.

William Temple says this:

> He showed both his hands and his side to them. It was proof of identity; this, however transmuted, was the Body which had hung on the Cross and was laid in the tomb. But the scars are more than this; they are the evidence not only that what they see is the Body of Jesus, but what is the quality for ever of the Body of Him whom they know with ever-deeper understanding as the Christ... The wounds of Christ are his credentials to the suffering race of men.

Yes, it is Jesus. He does give his peace. He also gives a task to be done, with the authority to do it. Jesus breathes on them, and they receive his life—his Spirit. At creation God breathed on man, and man became 'a living soul'. God's breath brings life to humankind. The 'dry bones' of Ezekiel's vision (Ezekiel 37) became alive and active when they received the breath of God. And men and women today can become new people; they too can know new life when they receive the life-giving Spirit of God through Jesus.

New life for all! But the old life has to be put off, discarded, so that the new life can flourish. 'Repent and believe' was, and is, the message. Jesus gave his friends the authority to pronounce the forgiveness of sin; not to forgive on their own account, but to pronounce to the penitent God's forgiveness.

Perhaps this has been misunderstood by many. The practice of confession and absolution is often wrongly seen as 'wiping the slate clean' by one mortal man for another, something a priest does for those who seek a new start; and the question is, 'How can this be so, when no one can forgive sins but God alone?' The answer is surely in these words of Jesus to his friends. He gives authority to remind those who do not recognize their sin that they are not forgiven until they honestly and truly admit their sin and their willingness to turn from it.

There are many who feel it is essential to confess their sins in the presence of a priest or minister, to hear the words of absolution and to receive a blessing. There are those who, knowing their need of forgiveness, seek counsel from a Christian friend who will be able to assure them through God's word in scripture that their sins are forgiven—for Jesus says they are, and his words are trustworthy and true. But no one has to go to a priest, a minister or a friend to receive that blessed assurance of forgiveness. They can simply ask Jesus, in the quietness of their own heart, and know the peace that comes through forgiveness, the new life of the Spirit.

However, I have found, as many others have done, that to be able to go to someone and share my guilt and repentance, to open my heart and to have that person assure me of the forgiveness of God, is an enormous relief and a means of blessing. William Barclay puts it like this:

> *This sentence does not mean that the power to forgive sins was ever entrusted to any man or to any men; it means that the power to proclaim that forgiveness was so entrusted; and it means that the power to warn that that forgiveness is not open to the impenitent was also entrusted to them. This sentence lays down the duty of the Church to convey forgiveness to the penitent in heart, and to warn the impenitent that they are forfeiting the mercy of God.*

For those friends of Jesus behind locked doors, their sadness was turned into joy, their fears dispelled, by this greeting: 'Peace'. But for one, it was too good to be true. One friend, Thomas, had not been with the others inside that locked room. He, in his grief, had done what many of us do when overcome with sadness; he had gone away to be on his own. He wanted no one but Jesus, and Jesus was dead. Yet no doubt, when he had poured out his grief, he then wanted to be with his friends, to comfort and help them, and so he went to them only to be astonished at the change in them.

They greeted him excitedly: 'We have seen the Lord!' They probably thought that Thomas would accept their word and rejoice with them—but not Thomas! He had experienced the depths of despair, had known the vain hope of it all being a nightmare, then the awakening to stark realization when he knew it was not a nightmare, it was terribly true. He recognized, too, that the mind can play tricks, and sadly he felt that his friends had been deluded.

There was only one way he could accept that Jesus was alive, and that was to touch him; for ghosts and figments of the imagination cannot be handled, but only real people. Of course, someone might have impersonated Jesus, but no one could fake those wounds. Thomas had seen the wounds inflicted—they were real, and the real Jesus would still carry them.

But was it possible that the message his friends so excitedly and confidently shared with him could be true? For a week they tried to convince him. For a week nothing happened. They met together again behind the locked doors, the only difference being that this time Thomas was with them. It must have been a week of argument, of exasperation at times—and could it have been that Thomas might have caused the others to doubt that previous experience? Did some of them begin to waver? Why were they still locking doors, if Jesus had really come to them? If it was true that he had given them peace and authority, why the locked doors again?

Into the locked room comes Jesus once more. Once more there is the greeting, 'Peace be with you!' And then, to Thomas, the invitation to discover for himself the living Lord Jesus, by touch. Thomas did not take up the invitation; he didn't need to any more. He knew beyond doubt that it was Jesus. And he knew something else—Jesus was not just his friend and leader, not only his Teacher and Master, but his Lord and his God. Thomas would never again doubt the risen Lord. He joined the ranks of those who have met personally with Jesus, Lord and God.

For two thousand years since, others, myself included, have met with that same Jesus, have accepted his forgiveness, his offer of new life, his authority, his Godhead. I have not seen him in the flesh as those first friends of his did; but I know him just the same as they did. I have been freed from fear, from sin, from weakness. I am no longer locked in by those things—for I have discovered, as Charles Wesley did, and described so graphically in his hymn:

> Long my imprisoned spirit lay
> Fast bound in sin and nature's night;
> Thine eye diffused a quickening ray,
> I woke, the dungeon flamed with light;
> My chains fell off, my heart was free,
> I rose, went forth and followed Thee.

For me, this is the happiness which Jesus promised to those who see him by faith. This promise he has kept, and will keep, until the day dawns when I, in company with all believers, will see him face to face, and enjoy his presence for all eternity.

# CHAPTER 23

# Gone fishing

## JOHN 21:1–14

Until about twenty years ago, my experience of fishing was restricted to memories of catching tiddlers in a net in the canal as a youngster, and trailing for mackerel on a trip round the bay in the summer. Then our teenage son was hit by the fishing bug in a big way. Over the following years, our home was gradually taken over by fishing gear, books and manuals, with unmentionables stored in the freezer for bait. He is now one of the country's leading experts on coarse fishing, his speciality being the carp. He fishes for carp, writes and lectures, edits magazines and conducts 'carp clinics'. He is so dedicated and enthusiastic that even I have become quite knowledgeable on the subject, having gone through twenty years of indoctrination on the joys of fishing. I even appear in his books, which is fair, as he does in mine. I tell him we are both in the fishing business: he fishes for carp, I fish for people.

I am glad my son is a fisherman, for he has an exacting and demanding job as a Senior Legal Officer working in the magistrates' court. Fishing helps him to unwind; it is a safety valve, a way for him to 'get away from it all'. Over the years I have become well used to finding a scribbled note, 'Gone fishing, love, Julian', and knowing that he will return tired, relaxed and happy after his time at the lake. Fortunately, too, he has an understanding girlfriend who recognizes his need to be out with his rods, for fishing is so much part of him.

The friends of Jesus had been through a most traumatic time. After the three hard years 'on the road' with him, they had lived through the despair and horror of his death, and the ecstasy of meeting him again after his resurrection. They had been commissioned by him for a life of service, sent out into the world to share the good news and to continue his work. Life was changing dramatically for them, almost minute by minute. They must have felt exhausted by the pressures, exhilarated and yet fearful, keyed up, wondering what on earth was going to happen to them next. It was all so new, they could hardly keep pace with the unfolding revelations.

Then, maybe, things went rather quiet. They were not sure what their next move should be; they had not yet found their feet—the Day of Pentecost was still in the future! They knew Jesus was alive. They had seen him, he had talked with them and given them their marching orders—but what should they be doing now?

Peter makes his mind up and announces he is going fishing! The others seize on it with enthusiasm; it is a good idea and they will go with him. So off they go on a fishing trip, just like the old days. Why did Peter suddenly decide to go fishing? Perhaps because, like my son when he has a lot on his mind and everything crowding in on him, he sought release in what he enjoyed and knew so well. Peter was a fisherman. It was his trade, it had been his life; and he felt safe and secure doing what he knew he was good at, using up the pent-up energy, getting to grips with the old life again.

The others jumped at the chance of getting out in a boat again, hoping to bring back a good catch, for they had to survive by their own means; they were not gentlemen with private incomes but working men—we often forget that. There was no Finance Committee behind them, no Church Commissioners sending a salary cheque at the end of each month—not even a Department of Social Security to help them out! So they set out on the fishing trip. They went at the right time, to the right place, with the right skills, and they caught... nothing.

I can imagine them, tired, dispirited, coming to the conclusion that they were a bunch of failures, wearily making their way back to shore with nothing to show for their night's work. And then someone shouts to them, asks them if they have caught anything. When they shout back, 'Not a thing', he tells them to try again, fishing this time from the other side of the boat. They respond to the stranger's instructions, to the note of authority in his voice. They do not question his advice, they just get on and follow it. To their delight and amazement, they find their nets full to bursting, so full in fact that they cannot haul them in; for probably by this time they were on the point of complete exhaustion.

John looks across, sees the man standing on the shore and suddenly realizes who it is. 'It's the Lord,' he says to Peter. And Peter, impetuous as ever, his tiredness disappearing at the mention of the Lord, jumps into the water, pulling his clothes on so as to be fit to meet his Master. There is work to do first, though; they have to get the catch and the boat to the shore. As they do so, they see that there is a fire burning. Jesus is waiting for them and asks them to bring him some of the fish they have caught.

When everything has been brought to land, the fish counted, the nets inspected and found intact, no breaks in them in spite of the huge catch, Jesus invites the men to eat the breakfast he has made ready. They are afraid to ask who he is, because they really know—it is Jesus who is here with them. And yet it seems so strange meeting him here; they are filled with a sense of awe and wonder. Then, as in the upper room only those few days ago, he hosts the meal with the food prepared by him especially for them.

Why did Jesus choose to meet them in this way, in such a commonplace situation? There they were, a bunch of fishermen returning after a night's fishing with nothing to show for their work. They would not have been expecting to see Jesus, probably not even thinking about him. They were too tired, too dispirited, to think about anything but getting their heads down. Yet Jesus was right there, turning their failure to success, providing just what they needed when they needed it.

I expect somehow to meet with Jesus when I am in church, at the big celebrations, as I meditate or read the Bible, or join in prayer with others. I do not really expect to meet him when I have just missed my train connection and the buffet bar is closed and I am sitting on a cold, draughty station. He is not uppermost in my thoughts when I am trying to get the car to start, and all I achieve is a dull rattle from the engine as it refuses to fire. Jesus is probably the last person I am thinking about as I frantically hunt for a piece of essential equipment when I was due at an appointment half an hour ago. And yet, over and over again, that's just when he does come, does speak, does provide me with what I need—be it patience, comfort, insight or a clear head. He sets me up again, gives me the encouragement I need to have another go and to get it right—he turns failure into success. I do not mean he waves a magic wand and all the troubles disappear, but he does get right alongside, showing me what really matters, helping me to focus straight again. Very ordinary practical things—but then, he is concerned with ordinary practical things, and with ordinary and often very impractical people!

As Jesus offered the bread and the fish to those hungry and tired friends on the shore of Lake Tiberias, the memories of past days must have come flooding back to them. They would remember the day Jesus fed the thousands with bread and fish, and how they were part of that miracle, distributing the food and clearing up afterwards. They would remember how he washed their feet before that last supper, and the bread and the wine they shared together. As they sat on the shore and munched their breakfast, they wouldn't feel much like talking, just being thankful, enjoying being together with him.

As I come to the Holy Communion service I am often reminded of past times, of special times, people and places. Each time I come with open hands to receive, it's a new experience of Jesus, and yet a reminder, too, of previous experiences. There isn't anything I have to say, but like the friends on the lake shore I know who it is who feeds me; I know it is the Lord, and I am so very, very thankful.

When Jesus, at the beginning of his ministry, called fishermen to come and follow him, he asked them to leave their old life behind, promising that he would teach them a new trade, catching people. They would be 'fishers of people'. That promise is to all who respond to Jesus, and who choose to follow him. We are all in the fishing business, once we follow Jesus. That's the job he entrusts to us, the task he empowers us to do. Fishing, as the friends found out earlier that night, and as all fishermen know, can be a pretty heartbreaking business. In spite of the effort, the skill, the equipment, sometimes there is nothing to show for all the hard work. Sometimes that experience can go on for a long time—I have seen many a dejected, weary fisherman plodding home empty-handed!

It is the same when we are fishing for humankind. We can put so much effort in, use all the right equipment, and still have nothing to show for it. It can go on year after year. I meet ministers and Christian workers who tell me so sadly, 'It's all been a waste of time my being in such-and-such a place.' Well, it's been said often, but it is worth repeating, that 'we are called to be faithful, not necessarily successful'. But failure does hurt!

Perhaps it is only as we lift our eyes from the failure, from our own feelings, our own frustration, that we will see someone in the distance making preparation for us, and we will know it is the Lord! It may be a long haul to the shore, but he will be there. He will be preparing for us, he will welcome us home; and it could be that we will find, to our surprise and joy, quite a catch in our net. One thing is sure, we will have everything we need when we sit down with our Lord in the kingdom of heaven.

# CHAPTER 24

# A new start in life

## JOHN 21:15-24

It was an ordinary scene, so very ordinary that you would not have given it a second glance. A boat pulled clear of the water, nets and catch ready for stowing away, and a group of fishermen lounging on the shore eating their breakfast, relaxing after a night's fishing before setting off home or to market. A fire burning, the smell of baked fish wafting across the shore, the low sound of voices. It was a commonplace scene along the shore of the lake. Two men were slightly detached from the group, and were in earnest conversation, perhaps discussing market prices, or whether to get a new boat. Or maybe it was something far more important than business transactions, for there was an intense sort of look about them; you could say they seemed to be 'out of this world'.

The place is the shore of Lake Tiberias, and Jesus, the risen Jesus, is talking with Peter. This is the first time Jesus and Peter have met in a 'one to one' situation since Jesus was arrested, before he was put to death. Peter had been with the others when he had come to them in the upper room, but he had just been one of a group; now Jesus wants to talk to Peter on his own. He has a great deal to say to him, but first a very searching question: 'Do you love me more than these others do?'

What a question! In the old days Peter would have flared up, reading into the words doubt about the superiority of his love. After all, he had always been first off the mark, the first one to declare passionately his love and commitment; but he had recently been proved sadly lacking. When challenged, he had denied he even knew Jesus. He was the one who looked back to the old life, who had 'taken to the boats' again. It was a very chastened Peter who replied, 'Yes, Lord, you know that I love you.' How could he dare to say that his love was stronger than anyone else's? Not now.

Some translations put the question 'Do you love me more than these?' interpreted as, 'Do you love me more than the old life?'—

more than being with your friends, more than being the 'boss' of the outfit?

However you read it, it is clear that Jesus is asking Peter if he puts him first in his life. Jesus asks him the question again—and then again for the third time. Poor Peter! He must have felt so awful remembering that he had actually denied Jesus three times, as Jesus had said he would; and now Jesus is digging into his heart, his will, his whole being. Dare he say he loves Jesus after what he has done? Can the old relationship of trust ever be restored? Does Jesus really believe him? At first, the original Greek makes clear, Peter dares only to reply that he loves Jesus as a friend. He cannot bring himself to claim to have that self-denying, total love that he once claimed—not because he does not feel it, but because he knows he did not attain it; he failed Jesus. His professed love was overcome by fear.

The second time he is asked, he can again only offer the love of a friend; but then Jesus comes down to his level, it seems, and asks him only if he is his friend. Peter can hardly reply, he is so full of sorrow, remorse, self-doubt. 'Lord, you know everything; you know I am!' The halting words from Peter's lips are of friendship, because he knows his past failures; his heart shouts his love in spite of them.

Jesus knew Peter all right. He knew his love and because he knew that love was real, he gave Peter the chance to declare it again. Much has been said and written concerning the threefold question, and it does seem that Jesus was giving Peter the chance to wipe out the past. Three times he had denied his Lord; three times he now affirms his love, and knows he is accepted. He has a new start, a new chance to prove his love.

How many times do you fail to live up to what you profess? I know I fail so often. It is easy to be bold when things are going well, easy when there is no opposition and we are riding along on the wave of success, ours or others', to profess our one hundred per cent dedication and love. It is often a different story when we are really pushed, when things go against us, when we are seemingly out of our depth; then we find ourselves going back on what we said with such fervour. Circumstances very often alter cases! Afterwards we could kick ourselves, we feel so ashamed—we, who thought we were so strong, have proved to be the weak link.

Then it is easy to accept defeat, accept ourselves as failures, and so give up; in effect, to go back to how things were before, like Peter did—to the old life. Yet Jesus knows our hearts. He knows whether our love is real or not. He knows our intention. He knows and understands, and gives us another chance—and another, and another! I have heard him speak those words to me after my failures: 'Margaret, do you love me?' I can only say with Peter, 'Lord, you know everything...'

As a self-confident teenager, I committed my life to the service of Jesus Christ. I promised my undying love. I would go anywhere, do anything; I would and I could! Three years later I had turned tail and sought pastures new—a better career, an easier life, good money, more time for myself. It was as a forty-year-old mother of two that I was again to hear the call to commitment, to love and to serve. As they say, 'a lot of water had flowed under a lot of bridges'. I was older. I knew myself a bit better. I did not so easily make declarations of undying love! Yet, as to Peter on the shore, came that insistent 'Do you love me more than these, than all this?' I could only say, 'Yes, the Lord being my helper'—and he has been. He has enabled me to express, at least in some measure, a degree of love and commitment. It is not one hundred per cent, I confess, but he and I are working on it together!

Peter found, when he again said 'I love you', that he was given a job to do for the one whom he claimed to love. He was to look after the lambs and the sheep, to care for them and to build them up—lambs and sheep of the human variety, who are much more difficult than any of the woolly-backed baa-ing sort!

For me, too, came the call to look after 'lambs' and 'sheep'; and sometimes I admit I would prefer those four-legged ones to the recalcitrant, wayward, obstinate and yet so loving and affectionate human ones I am called to care for; who take up so much time, who make so many demands, and who in the end often wander off and do their own thing! Yet, as I look back on my life, I am so grateful to many who had heard the words of Jesus to 'take care of my lambs, take care of my sheep' and who cared for me, from the frisky lamb stage right through to the 'so set in her ways' sheep! I am thankful for those who still persevere with me—I am sure that, had I been a sheep, I would have been consigned to the meat pie factory long ago!

Being an under-shepherd is the most rewarding and exciting life. Seeing the lambs grow up, the flock increase—no, I wouldn't exchange my life for any other! Who knows what may happen in the future; what demands the ministry will make upon me? There may come a time when I am forced into a situation I just don't want to be in; but then that is the risk I have to take, just as every other minister has had to take it since Peter was warned of the cost of being a shepherd.

Peter is forgiven for the past and recommissioned for the future, as Jesus says again those words, 'Follow me.' It is to an older, wiser Peter that the call comes now. He has had to learn the hard way what following Jesus is all about, yet what experiences he has shared in, witnessed for himself; what unique privileges he has enjoyed! Now the call comes again, and he sets off to follow his calling, even to the death. But first there comes a moment when he looks behind him, and sees John, 'the disciple whom Jesus loved'. Does a flicker of resentment or envy pass through Peter's mind as he remembers how special John has always been to Jesus, as he asks, 'Lord, what about this man?'—a touch of the old Peter!

Jesus firmly replies to Peter's question by telling him to mind his own business! What John or anyone else had to do, where they had to go, the end they would meet, was between the individual concerned and Jesus, not anyone else. Peter had his instructions; he was to get on with following them out. Whether John lived a long or short time, whether he would still be around when Jesus returned again; that was not Peter's or anyone else's concern. Of course there were those who misinterpreted the words of Jesus, who read into them something that was not there; but hasn't it always been so! Death came sooner to one and later to the other, but who is to say who had the greater ministry? Peter, who died a violent death like his Master, or John, who lived on into old age in exile?

In spite of hearing the words, 'Follow me', and setting out willingly to do so, I suppose we all glance over our shoulder at times to see what 'the others' are up to! 'What about him? What about her?' we all want to know, don't we? I know I do! As I pose that question to Jesus, he gives me a tug: 'Come on, this way, never mind about anyone else!' I obey—for a while; and then ask the same question—and get the same answer!

So I follow on, sometimes rushing and jumping, eager and confident. At other times I drag my feet, dig my heels in, look backwards, but I keep hearing those words: 'Follow me!' And when I hear them, I know who it is who is calling. I know his voice. I know that he loves me, that he is my 'good shepherd'. And so I go on answering: 'I'm coming, I'm on my way. Don't let me go, will you?'—and I know for sure that he will never let me go, never let me down, and never let me off the path he has set for me. And what a relief it is to know that!

*O Jesus, Thou has promised*
*To all who follow Thee*
*That where Thou art in glory*
*There shall Thy servant be;*
*And, Jesus, I have promised*
*To serve Thee to the end!*
*O give me grace to follow,*
*My Master and my Friend.*

**J.E. Bode (1816–74)**

# So where does that leave you?

## JOHN 21:25

Why did John write this account of the life and death of Jesus? Why did he record events, relationships, conversations, the lives of so many people? Why did he give such minute details, almost 'asides', when he described the greatest event in history, the resurrection from the dead of Jesus? Why did he include some things and leave out others? After all, he gives us only a thumbnail sketch. Jesus must have said and done literally thousands of things more than have been recorded by John, or any of the other Gospel writers.

John gives the answer quite clearly:

> *In his disciples' presence Jesus performed many other miracles which are not written down in this book. But these have been written in order that you may believe that Jesus is the Messiah, the Son of God, and that through your faith in him you may have life.*

> ### John 20:30

So never mind what has not been put down; there is no need to worry about that which we do not possess. There is all we need in John's account to come to know Jesus for ourselves, to realize just who he is, what he has done and what he offers. There is enough here for anyone!

So, then, you could ask, why have I been bold enough to try to explain and put into contemporary language what John was talking about in the last eleven chapters of his Gospel account? After all, Margaret Cundiff is no theologian—she possesses the minimum of qualifications; she gained no glittering prizes for academic excellence; she is a very average, ordinary, middle-aged woman, living in a very average, ordinary, middle-aged situation. Two thousand years separate her from the things she describes. Yet do they?

I have found these chapters of John's Gospel completely relevant to my life today. It has been as though I had been grasped by the scruff of the neck and made to watch, listen and be part of the scene. Not as an idle spectator, but as someone who must respond by taking either the way of life or the way of death.

The words of John's Gospel are beautiful, but the danger is that they can become just beautiful well-known prose, so familiar that they run off the tongue and away, without ever touching our lives. I have tried to stand with them, to be part of them, to respond to them. As I have done this, I have found I have been challenged over and over again by my own lifestyle, by my sometimes second-hand views. I have also seen how my own personal life experiences are part and parcel of my attitude to Jesus. Sometimes these experiences and feelings have had to be broken by him so that I might receive the living bread, and not yesterday's stale crusts.

John ends the Gospel account with these words: 'Now, there are many other things that Jesus did. If they were all written down one by one, I suppose the whole world could not hold the books that would be written.' Jesus has gone on doing things since John finished his Gospel account—wonderful things, breathtaking, glorious things, changing people's lives, transforming situations, bringing comfort, hope, strength and new life in situations and places from one end of the earth to the other. John was right: the world could not contain all the books that would be needed to record the doings of Jesus, for he is still doing them!

This book is my book—you could call it 'the good news according to Margaret Cundiff'—and I tell you this, it is all true!

So where does that leave you?

Only you can answer that question. But my advice is that you take up the challenge of Jesus, as he says to you, today, right now: 'Follow me.'

You may be interested to know that Margaret Cundiff is a regular contributor to BRF's popular series of Bible reading notes, *New Daylight*. *New Daylight* is ideal for those looking for a fresh, devotional approach to reading and understanding the Bible. Each issue covers four months of daily Bible reading and reflection with each day offering a Bible passage (text included), helpful comment and a prayer or thought for the day ahead.

Edited by David Winter, an Anglican priest in the Diocese of Oxford he is former BBC Head of Religious Broadcasting at the BBC, he is a regular contributor to Thought for the Day and Prayer for Today. *New Daylight* is written by a gifted team of contributors including Adrian Plass, Brother Ramon, Hilary McDowell, Marcus Maxwell, Margaret Cundiff, Henry Wansbrough, Rosemary Green, Rob Gillion, Graham Dodds and Peter Graves.

New Daylight is also available in large print and on cassette for the visually impaired.

## NEW DAYLIGHT SUBSCRIPTIONS

❏ I would like to give a gift subscription
(please complete both name and address sections below)
❏ I would like to take out a subscription myself
(complete name and address details only once)

This completed coupon should be sent with appropriate payment to BRF. Alternatively, please write to us quoting your name, address, the subscription you would like for either yourself or a friend (with their name and address), the start date and credit card number, expiry date and signature if paying by credit card.

Gift subscription name _____

Gift subscription address _____

_____ Postcode _____

**Please send to the above, beginning with the May 2000 issue:**

| (please tick box) | UK | SURFACE | AIR MAIL |
|---|---|---|---|
| NEW DAYLIGHT | ❏ £10.20 | ❏ £11.55 | ❏ £13.50 |
| NEW DAYLIGHT 3-year sub | ❏ £25.00 | | |

Please complete the payment details below and send your coupon, with appropriate payment to: **The Bible Reading Fellowship, Peter's Way, Sandy Lane West, Oxford OX4 5HG**

Your name _____

Your address _____

_____ Postcode _____

Total enclosed £ _____ (cheques should be made payable to 'BRF')

Payment by cheque ❏ postal order ❏ Visa ❏ Mastercard ❏ Switch ❏

Card number: ☐☐☐☐ ☐☐☐☐ ☐☐☐☐ ☐☐☐☐

Expiry date of card: ☐☐☐☐ Issue number (Switch): ☐☐☐☐

Signature (essential if paying by credit/Switch card) _____

NB: BRF notes are also available from your local Christian bookshop.    **BRF is a Registered Char**

# Also by Margaret Cundiff

## *Something for the Journey*

'The title for this book was inspired by memories of gifts given to me over the years, tokens of love pressed into my hands by parents, friends, colleagues and even complete strangers as I set off on a journey. These gifts encouraged, comforted and sustained me, not just by what they were, but by the reminder of the givers and our relationship.

'In the Bible I have found many gifts, placed into my hands and heart by God, as "something for the journey". These gifts are reminders of his love, concern, expectations and promises, sustaining me through this life to the joys of the next. I would like to share with you some of these treasures, to help you on your own journey, speak to you afresh of the joy of God's word, and encourage you to venture into new territory, into a deeper relationship with him.'

## *Living by the Book*
### *A personal journey through the Sermon on the Mount*

'If everybody lived by the Sermon on the Mount,' said the man on the train, 'the world would be a better place.'

This remark started Margaret Cundiff on a journey of exploration to rediscover those chapters of Matthew's Gospel that we think we know so well. It was, she found, a sometimes risky process, challenging our most basic assumptions about how we live our lives, and demanding honest answers to hard questions.

Join Margaret in discovering what Jesus really says about the good life, and what it involves for those who set out to follow him. Is it possible for ordinary Christians to live by the Book? What happens if we don't? What happens if we do?

*See overleaf for an order form for both books.*